Anna Morton

Chinese Cresteds

Everything About Purchase, Care, Nutrition, Grooming, and Health

Filled with Full-color Photographs
Illustrations by Pam Tanzey

BARRON'S

CONTENTS

INTRODUCING THE CHINESE CRESTED

Is it a cat, a rat, or a monkey?
No, it is the Chinese Crested dog!
Straight from Fairyland, the
Chinese Crested shares the
same mythical background
as the Hydra and the Sphinx.

The Legendary Past of the Chinese Crested

Hairless dogs seem to have arisen by mutation all over the world, but they have been found principally in Central and South America. The written history of the breed began in the 1500s.

Besides the Chinese Crested dog, there are at least 26 hairless breeds in the world. Among them are the better-known Elephant Dog from Africa, which is one of the largest, the hairless Mexican Xoloitzcuintli, and the Moonflower from Peru. Some of the names that have been given to the Chinese Crested are Chinese Hairless, Chinese Ship Dog, and Chinese Royal Hairless. In Egypt this dog is called the Pyramid or Giza Hairless; in South Africa, the South

The Chinese Crested is considered one of the most graceful and elegant of breeds.

African Hairless; and in Turkey, the Turkish Hairless. But the best known is the Chinese Crested.

Why the name *Chinese Crested*? Most likely, the name is derived from the 16th-century Chinese seafarers who sailed the high seas with the breed on board and popularized them as rat catchers, trading them with local merchants at port cities. In this way, the breed was distributed throughout Turkey, Egypt, South Africa, and Asia.

Hairless dogs were bred for thousands of years for companionship, hunting, and food. Judging by the archaeological evidence, the hairless mutation occurred in Mexico either before or around 1500 B.C.

Dogs are not the only species to be affected with the hairless mutation. There is plenty of evidence of hairless horses, guinea pigs, cats, and even mice. Japanese myths mention hairless foxes. In Eskimo belief, Qiqirn is a spirit

There are at least 26 hairless breeds in the world.

of mulberries from another, and 300 hairless dogs—supposedly a great delicacy.

Native Nicaraguans believe that hairless dogs know and can speak the language of the gods. Folk legend has it that a great dog found its way from the underworld and was born out of a volcano. This dog is believed to forever have the burned skin it received from the volcano, and this is why it is now hairless.

Historically in Mexico and South America there have always been several types of hairless dogs, including the coated members of the groups. The most common is the Mexican Hairless. These small dogs are presumably the original hairless types in Mexico, as shown by old Colima pottery. The Mexican Hairless is thought to originate from the *pila* group of hairless canines. The name *pila* signifies a native hairless dog found in several South American countries, especially Peru, Argentina, and Bolivia.

Most likely, the Chinese Crested originated from the Mexican Hairless gene pool by the selective breeding of the dogs with the pila genes that had the desired long crest. This has led to the type being considered a separate breed with an apparently stable gene pool.

After the Spanish Conquest, the reverence for the hairless dogs in Mexico and South America disappeared, and the dogs became forgotten until they reappeared in Europe in the 1800s.

who appears in the shape of a huge, hairless dog. Qiqirn is described as having hair only on its mouth, feet, ears, and tail tip.

Nevertheless, it was mostly hairless dogs and cats that were maintained systematically to ensure continuity of their kind.

The 16th-century Aztecs, who were the successors to the Toltecs, venerated hairless dogs. The priests from the Cholula temple were famous for breeding purple-skinned dogs for sacrificial purposes.

In 1540, Hernando de Soto's expedition passed through the outskirts of Cherokee territory. According to the Spanish chroniclers on the expedition, the Cherokee villages provided food: 700 turkeys from one village, 20 baskets

Modern History

By the mid-19th century, pictures of the Chinese Crested began to emerge in numerous paintings and prints in Europe. The first pair of

Chinese Crested dogs brought to London in the 1860s came as part of a zoological show.

With the introduction of dog shows in the 1800s, Chinese Cresteds began participating in competition. In Great Britain, the first Chinese Crested dog was registered in 1881, and eventually the United Kennel Club recognized the breed on January 1, 1995.

In the United States, the Chinese Crested variety enjoyed a short stay in the American Kennel Club (AKC) Miscellaneous class and was exhibited in 1885 at Westminster.

In 1880, Ida Garrett, a writer from New York, became involved with the breed. In 1920 she met another Crested enthusiast, Debra Woods, and for nearly 40 years these two women worked together to promote the Chinese Crested breed in the United States.

Woods, whose kennel's name was Crest-Haven, kept a detailed record of all her dogs, beginning in the 1930s. In the 1950s, her breeding records and studbook became extensive enough to start the American Hairless Dog Club as a registration service for Chinese Cresteds. The club started in March 1959, with only two members. However, the membership grew fast, and in four years Woods had registered 160 Chinese Cresteds and 200 Mexican Hairless.

Gypsy Rose Lee, a famous stripper, was one of the first serious Crested breeders. Her sister had rescued a Chinese Crested dog from a Connecticut animal shelter and had given it to Gypsy to include in her act. The publicity she created

Today, nearly all Chinese Crested bloodlines in the world can trace the lineage of their dogs to Debra Woods (Crest-Haven) and Gypsy Rose Lee (Lee) lines.

The breed consists of two varieties: a coated and a hairless.

eventually brought the Chinese Crested to the attention of the public.

In October 1978 the American Chinese Crested Club was founded. In 1986, the breed found its place in the Miscellaneous classes of the American Kennel Club. Finally, in 1991, the American Chinese Crested Club was officially invited to join the American Kennel Club.

Since its acceptance into the American Kennel Club, the Chinese Crested dog has been participating in many title events, such as obedience, agility trials, and confirmation competitions. Many Chinese Cresteds have become outstanding therapy or guide dogs. Some have achieved movie stardom by appearing in popular films

Chargi's PS of Phaedrian was the first World Champion and the most titled dog in the Crested breed.

and TV shows. The breed is becoming more popular each year, providing joyful companionship for adults and children alike. However, the breed is not for everyone, and poor understanding of the dog's temperament and needs is often a major reason why Crested rescue organizations have their hands full and why owners tire of their intelligent but stubborn pets.

The Nature of the Chinese Crested Dog

Often the first impression people will have upon meeting your Hairless Crested puppy is:

Both varieties of Chinese Cresteds need to be in homes where the owners can devote a lot of time to them.

"Oh, my, what happened to its coat?" Powderpuffs, which are groomed to look like miniature Afghans, are great attention magnets as well. Although it is true that Chinese Cresteds often make fantastic pets, it is also true that they require a lot of care and understanding from their owners. These are not dogs that can be left at home for many hours. When alone, Cresteds, particularly the Hairless variety, can become very unhappy, destructive, or sick. Powderpuff dogs are somehow more emotionally balanced than Hairless dogs, but it does not mean that they are less sensitive.

Your Chinese Crested will thrive on love, but at the same time she is always ready to offer much in return. Because of their constant desire to bond with their owners, these dogs can be especially jealous of anyone competing for affection. For that reason, they are not always the best choice for a home with small children, with whom they may compete for a parent's love. With older children, there is rarely a problem, because most Cresteds will try to bond with them first before seeking affection from their parents.

Inquisitive and playful, your Chinese Crested puppy is famous for her intelligence. In fact, Chinese Cresteds are very perceptive when it comes to recognizing and interpreting human behavior. Their uncanny ability to read human body language makes them loyal protectors, ready to defend their owners with their lives.

The Chinese Crested loves to climb and jump, and no height is too high, something that, of course, may end with a broken leg and often does. Climbing fences and tables is a favorite sport of many Cresteds. They also love to vocalize loudly with a variety of howls and barks, especially when left alone at home.

Chinese Cresteds considers themselves children of their owners and demand to be treated as such. When sleeping in her owner's bed, the dog will usually take the uppermost position, often on top of "mom's" or "dad's" head.

It must be said, though, that the breed is, on

The Hairless variety seems to have a "catlike" character and will do things such as curl up in your lap or around your neck. The Powderpuff is more likely to stay at your feet and seems more "doglike" in character.

average, hard to housebreak, and for this reason every Crested should be trained as early as possible to behave properly at home.

Both varieties of the Chinese Crested are very active dogs and benefit from obedience and agility training. This prevents boredom, to which they are highly prone. A well-trained Crested dog can be a pleasure to have around, something that cannot be said about a poorly behaved dog with uncontrolled housebreaking habits or behavioral problems. Males need to be neutered by the seventh month at the latest, and females spayed by the ninth month. Great success has also been accomplished with earlier surgeries,

A shaved Powderpuff next to a Hairless.

A true Hairless Crested is now rarely seen at competition events.

even as early as six weeks. You should talk with your veterinarian about these options and decide what is most appropriate for the dog's needs.

Chinese Cresteds, if not socialized early in life, may grow up to become aloof, unfriendly, or even aggressive. The well-bred Chinese Crested is normally very friendly with other dogs and pets, and loves to be the center of attention.

Many Chinese Crested dogs, after undergoing special training, have become successful service dogs, providing assistance to an individual with a disability. Many owners swear that their Chinese Crested has special healing powers and that contact with their warm, soft skin can cure headaches and a variety of other ailments, such as rheumatism.

This breed is also exceptionally good for apartment dwelling and can be taught to use a litter box if necessary.

Both varieties of Chinese Crested love to play a lot, sometimes roughly. To protect them from injuries, special attention should be given to make sure they do not jump or run into walls.

The color of your Chinese Crested dog's skin can range from pink to black, and includes plum, mahogany, blue, silver, pale mauve, or copper. Many are born pink, only to change color later. A puppy born black may fade to blue, and the silver puppy can turn red. The dogs either are of a uniform color or spotted.

The Hairless Chinese Crested's skin needs to be cared for on a regular basis. The Hairless variety is also sensitive to cold and vulnerable to extreme weather. A wardrobe of appropriate dog clothing is a must for the summer to protect their skin from sunburn and for the winter to keep them warm.

The Powderpuff's coat needs just as much care as the skin of the Hairless type. The Pow-

The Chinese Crested portrait.

derpuff should be brushed daily, with close attention paid to its undercoat to prevent matting. Because this breed sheds little or no hair, it is a good choice for people who suffer from allergies. The breed is also relatively odorless.

The average lifespan of the breed is 13 to 15 years.

Two Varieties in One Litter

The breed is represented by two varieties: a Hairless dog looking like a small pony or a deer, and a coated type (Powderpuff). The Powderpuff is not born hairless, and will not carry hairless genes.

How hairless is a Hairless dog? The amount of body hair will differ. All have some hair on the head, tail, and feet. Some also have shorter or longer hair on the ears, and often they will have a fuzzy face. Some Hairless dogs will have only a little soft, downy fuzz on their bodies, whereas others will be very hairy, looking almost like shorthair terriers. However, even the very hairy Crested Hairless will be still considered hairless genetically if the hairless genes are present.

The Hairless Chinese Crested often has long hair flowing from her head and a moplike tail. When shaved and groomed properly, hairy Hairless dogs will present a picture of perfection with their profuse crests, thick socks, tail plumes, and long, majestically hanging ear fringes. True Hairless dogs usually have very sparse furnishings, often amounting to not more than a little crest and a touch of hair on their feet and tails. A crest and the other furnishings may take many months to reach full length, particularly in the true hairless dog.

Although they may not look as glamorous as their hairy littermates, who must be shaved for the hairless look, their soft, naturally naked warm skin is a pleasure to touch. In addition, the little or no grooming required is an extra plus in having a true hairless dog.

The Powderpuff Chinese Crested has a long, voluminous, and preferably silky coat that, when properly groomed, can appear to look like a miniature Afghan Hound. The coat can be of any color, but white is the most common.

At birth, Powderpuff puppies can look almost indistinguishable from their hairy Hairless littermates. Sometimes the only difference is the missing hair on the abdominal area and inner thighs of the Hairless newborns.

Inquisitive and playful, the Chinese Crested dog is famous for her intelligence.

Both varieties can be born with extra dewclaws on their rear legs, and these need to be removed by the seventh day after birth.

Genetics

Like all mammals (including humans), dogs inherit their physical characteristics from both of their parents. These characteristics are called genes. Each dog has thirty-nine genes, and one of each pair is inherited from each parent.

Research pertaining to the breeding of hairless dogs indicates that hairlessness is caused by a dominant gene. However, every Hairless Chinese Crested carries not only the (H) dominant hairless gene, but also the (h) recessive gene for hair. Thus, all Chinese Cresteds carry at least one copy of the Powderpuff allele. It is also believed that the HH combination (homozygous) is lethal. Any puppy with a double Hairless gene will either be born dead or die soon after birth. Because only Hh-carrying dogs

survive and can be bred, every Hairless dog can produce a coated and a Hairless offspring in the same litter. Presence of the lethal gene explains why it is impossible to produce only Hairless offspring and breed out the coated variety.

The Hairless gene is linked with missing and abnormally shaped teeth. The canine teeth in a Hairless variety tend to point forward like tusks. This appearance may not be so dramatic in hairy Hairless dogs; nevertheless, to an experienced eye, it is easily detectable.

The average owner should not attempt breeding Chinese Cresteds without first acquiring a basic knowledge of genetics.

The General Chinese Crested Standard

The confirmation or structure of the Chinese Crested dog, or any dog for that matter, plays an inherent role in its ability to overcome obstacles and maintain balance, form, and function.

A fine-boned and slender dog, the Chinese Crested should be slightly longer than it is tall. Its legs are long and straight. In the Hairless variety, the feet are narrow and harelike, with elongated toes. The wedge-shaped head has almond-shaped eyes that are set wide, and they offer an intense and alert expression. The eye color should be either black or brown, or reflect the overall dog's pigmentation. A palomino-colored dog may have hazel, green, or yellow eyes.

The large ears are not cropped and sit erect, so that the base of the ear is level with the outside corner of the eye. The cheeks should taper smoothly into the muzzle, which features a preferably solidly pigmented nose. The teeth must meet in either a scissors or level bite. Missing teeth in the Powderpuff are considered

When in full coat, the Chinese Crested Powderpuff can shine as one of the most elegant looking of toy dogs.

a fault. The neck is lean and slightly arched from the withers to the base of the head.

The tail is slender, tapering to a small curve at the end and long enough to reach the hock. At movement, the tail is carried high, resembling a sickle. In the Hairless variety, two-thirds of the tail is covered with hair. A tail that is short, curly, or bends to the side is considered a fault.

Layback of shoulders should be at 45 degrees. Shoulders should be close to the body and nicely rounded, never flat.

The topline should be flat or slightly slanted. The brisket extends to the elbow. The breastbone should not be prominent or sticking out, and the ribs should be well developed. The depth of the chest goes to a moderate tuck at the flanks.

The Hairless variety features soft and silky hair on certain portions of the body, including the head (crest), the tail (plume), and the feet (socks). The hairless portions of the body are soft and smooth. The amount of crest and furnishings is usually relative to the amount of body hair a dog possesses. As a rule, the more hairy the dog, the more profuse are its furnishings. Skin ought to be free of blemishes and have an attractive appearance.

The coat of the Powderpuff variety features a soft double coat over the entire body. The hair is straight and moderately long and dense. A kinky or curly coat is incorrect and is to be penalized at shows.

The ideal size is 12 inches (30 cm) when measured from the tip of the shoulder blade to the ground. In reality, most Chinese Cresteds are between 11 and 13 inches (28–32.5 cm),

although slightly smaller or larger size is permitted. The weight varies, but usually it is about 7 pounds (3 kg) for a dog 10 to 11 inches (25–28 cm) tall and should not be more than 12 pounds (5 kg) for one 13 inches (32.5 cm) long measured by height.

The Chinese Crested's gait is smooth and graceful. It should exhibit good reach in the forequarters and good drive in the hindquarters. While the dog is trotting, the topline remains firm and level. In the show ring, the Chinese Crested should be moved on a loose lead at a moderately fast trot. The overall impression is that of a well-balanced rectangle on four strong, well-positioned legs.

The American Standard differs only slightly from the European Standard. For additional information, see the contact addresses that are provided in "Information."

The American Chinese Crested Standard requires that the varieties, the Powderpuff and the Hairless, have erect ears. In Europe, Canada, and some other countries, the Standard is more forgiving in regards to the ears of the Powderpuff, but not to the ears of the Hairless. Yet not every Chinese Crested is born with erect ears. In many cases, the ears have to be trained to stand. The ear-training routine should begin when the puppy is still very young and the ear cartilage is intact, because once it breaks from repeated creasing and folding, it may be impossible to correct the problem. This may not be an issue for the pet Chinese Crested, but for a show-prospect puppy it means a career that is finished before it is even started. The simplest way to train ears to stand is to tape them with cotton tape. A standard porous cotton tape, 1 inch (2.5 cm) wide, is preferred because it allows for air circulation. Two pieces of tape are cut, each about 4 inches (10 cm) long. The ears are stretched up and taped flat across, back and front.

Another method consists of wrapping the ears. Cotton batting is rolled into a rod about 1/3 inch (8 mm) wide and slightly shorter than the length of the ear. Tampons make great rods, as do Popsicle sticks, tongue depressors, or foam posts. The rods are inserted into the dog's ears, and then the ears are stretched out and curled around them. Next, a 4-inch (10-cm) piece of tape is wrapped around, starting from the bottom and coming around the ear, making sure that the ear is stretched up well. Both ears must be vertically straight. To form a bridge, another piece of tape, about 10 inches (25 cm) long, is needed. The bridge is made by attaching one end of the tape to one ear, extending the tape over the head and wrapping it around the other ear, then coming back to the first ear and again across to the other ear. The tape's folds above the head are later pinched, sticky side to sticky side, thus forming a bridge, which holds both ears in an upright position.

The tape should stay on the ears for four to five days and then be taken off to prevent infection. After the tape is taken off, the ears are left to rest for a day and the procedure should be repeated the next day.

You will need to regularly check the ears for any signs of inflammation. If the ears become red or swollen, you will need to remove the tape immediately, wash the ears gently with soapy water, dry the ears gently, and apply antibiotic cream to the surface. The ear will need to rest for a while until it heals completely. Prior to re-taping the ear, it is very important to shave the hair off the ears before each taping procedure, as hair on the ear adds weight, making the training process longer. Also, removing hair from the sticky tape can be very painful to the dog.

It is not advisable to use Nair or other hair removers, as the skin on the ear is very fragile and sensitive, and can easily become inflamed from chemicals present in commercial preparations.

Ears are taped across with cotton tape.

EARS TO STAND UP

Using a Wahl hand trimmer with the #40 blade is a better option, although you still need to be careful not to accidentally cut the delicate ear edge when shaving. If you are inexperienced with a trimmer, be aware that the blade is sharp, so first practice on yourself or on an old piece of fur before trying to trim your dog's ears. After shaving the ears, wash them well with soap, as oily skin or presence of hair debris will prevent proper sticking of the tape. Once the ears are completely dry, you can apply the adhesive as first described.

Another popular ear-training method consists of making a paper form and attaching it with the skin bond to the ear. The paper form, slightly smaller than the size of the ear, is cut from a brown shopping bag. The dog's ears must be thoroughly cleaned with rubbing alcohol or the form will not adhere properly. The glue is brushed on one side of the form and on the inside of the dog's ear and allowed to thicken for a few seconds for better adherence. The form is next pressed against the ear and held in position until dry. The same is done with the other ear.

After four or five days, the form is removed, the ears are cleaned with alcohol, and after a short rest, the whole procedure is repeated. The owner must be very careful not to allow the glue or alcohol to drip into the ear, because this can injure the eardrum.

The taping must be done consistently until the ears are standing. This sometimes means taping the ears for a year or even longer!

If, in spite of your most diligent efforts, the Crested's ears still won't stand, this could be due to the following causes:
• The dog has inherited a gene for soft ears.
• The ear cartilage has suffered some damage.

Nothing can be done if the cause is genetic. Cartilage damage is usually caused by puppies tugging and pulling on each others ears. Broken

Ears are rolled around cotton rods and joined by a tape bridge across the head.

cartilage is the most common reason and, unfortunately, often permanent.

Another possibility is that the puppy hasn't matured enough. During the teething period, the organisms' dependency on calcium and zinc often exceeds the supply, and floppy ears are a common result. In this situation, you need to be patient. Once the adult teeth come in, the problem should resolve itself.

Some veterinarian's advise adding a zinc and calcium/phosphorus combination to the dog's diet during the teething period. In this author's opinion, adding silica and glucosamine supplements may also help to strengthen the ears. Some breeders desperate to win in the show ring occasionally lower themselves to having the ears surgically altered, which consist of inserting steel wires into the ears to make them stand. However, this procedure is not only against AKC and most other canine organizations' rules, but is also very painful to the dog. In addition, one cannot cheat genes and, if the dog is bred, the same problem will occur in his/her offspring.

CHOOSING THE CHINESE CRESTED

Pink or blue, a boy or a girl, a Hairless or a Puff, spotted or solid color, a puppy or an adult . . . choosing the right Chinese Crested can be as hard as trying to find the best-tasting candy in Willy Wonka's Chocolate Factory.

Selecting the Variety: Hairless or Powderpuff?

Most people become attracted to the Chinese Crested dog because they are fascinated with the Hairless variety. Not many are aware of the coated dogs born in the same litter, and when they see a Hairless dog next to its Powderpuff brother, they assume that it is a different breed. Although the two dogs will look structurally the same, there are some differences. The most important, of course, is that a Hairless dog is a mutation, whereas a Powderpuff carries the original genes of the breed's ancestors.

The Hairless mutation also influences other genes. Thus, Hairless dogs have feet with long toes that are used like a hand. Another important difference is misshapen or missing teeth

The Hairless Crested has a very distinct skin from a Powderpuff.

and short teeth roots. It is rare for a Hairless to keep its teeth intact to old age.

Also, the Hairless Crested's skin is very distinct from that of a Powderpuff. The skin, despite its delicate or fragile look, is tough, almost as tough as an elephant's. Unfortunately, it is also prone to dermatological problems and bacterial contamination or yeast.

Some Hairless dogs possess skin so sensitive that they will respond to a touch as if to pain. They can also shiver a lot and get nervous when stroked or petted. For this reason, they need to be handled very gently.

One of the unique characteristics you'll find of your Hairless Crested is that he possesses sweat glands. In fact, among all canine breeds, only hairless dogs sweat. This feature makes your puppy vulnerable to dehydration and requires that you provide the dog with a readily available source of fresh water all the time.

**A potential owner of a Chinese Crested
needs to be prepared for a life
of long-term skin care.**

Any idea that a Hairless dog is maintenance-free must be abandoned as a fantasy. It must also be stressed that the average Chinese Crested is very emotionally dependent on its owner, so a Chinese Crested may not be the best choice for a person who must work long hours or is unable to give him enough care or individual attention. Food allergies and wardrobe needs also make the Chinese Crested an expensive pet, beyond the means of many families.

In comparison, the Powderpuff dog has lesser needs. A Powderpuff's coat needs only minimal regular grooming to look attractive. In addition, an owner who gets tired of the grooming hassle can always shave the Powderpuff down to resemble the Hairless. Of course, a show prospect will require more extensive coat care, but the same applies to the Hairless dog.

When in full coat, the Chinese Crested Powderpuff can shine as one of the most elegant looking of toy dogs. The dog's coat should resemble a powder puff that women use cosmetically. It is straight, of moderate density and length. A close look reveals long, thin guard hairs over a short silky undercoat.

Compared with the Hairless Crested, the Powderpuff is also relatively easy to train and housebreak. A nonshedding coat makes the dog an excellent choice for allergy sufferers. However, this should not be taken for granted, as in severe cases, even Hairless dogs can trigger an asthma attack. If a person suffers from allergies, it is always best to meet a dog in person, either at a dog show or by visiting a breeder, and monitor any allergic reaction.

Apartment dwellers should be aware that the Chinese Crested dog is very vocal and that its howling can be disruptive to neighbors. Although it is mainly the Hairless Cresteds who howl, the Powderpuffs are known to do so as well, although not so loudly. Their vocalization is more like singing than howling. Both varieties tend to bark frequently.

Puppy or Adult Dog?

Most people who want the Chinese Crested dog for a companion seek a young puppy, either in the belief that he will be more malleable when it comes to training or because they are attracted to the puppy's temporary charm. Some think it is easier to bond with a young puppy than with an older dog.

Impulsive attraction is always a wrong reason to buy a pet, but the other reasons have some element of truth. Sometimes older dogs have a harder time adjusting to a new environment or bonding with a new owner. However, there are no rules here, and much depends on the character of the dog in question.

Some Chinese Cresteds can be very stubborn as puppies, thus requiring a prolonged training routine and much socializing. Many older dogs, however, who are usually already housebroken and socialized by the breeder, will have no difficulty adjusting to a new home, even welcoming it as a haven from the breeder's household of many dogs.

When choosing your pet, the Chinese Crested puppy should not be selected earlier than eight weeks and then only after being checked for hidden defects and evaluated for temperament. A show prospect should not be offered for sale or bought before reaching at least 12–14 weeks of age, unless a person is experienced enough in judging dogs to recognize quality at an earlier age. Otherwise, the ideal age to buy a show prospect is at four or five months. By this time most defects will have appeared, and it will be possible to make a reasonable prediction about the pup's mature size, evaluate temperament and confirmation, and perform CERF (Canine Eye Registration Foundation) and OFA (Orthopedic Foundation for Animals) tests.

Male or Female?

Many people believe that a female is cleaner, gentler, and would make a better pet. Although this may be true with some breeds, Chinese Crested males can make as good, if not better, pets than females, particularly if a puppy is neutered before reaching its full sexual maturity, which usually takes place around five to seven months. Removal of the testicles before complete development will prevent the male puppy from asserting his stud character in such dominant acts as urine marking, fecal signaling, or aggressive behavior. A neutered male will be inclined to act more in a puppylike manner, be more gentle, and try to take care of his own hygiene. He will also appreciate more readily any cleaning routine offered by the owner. Neutered males also have less body odor and are less prone to skin eruptions, which are often triggered by hormonal surges.

Nevertheless, even intact males can make fantastic pets. Some act very lovingly, wanting to cozy up with their owners at all times. Some males are so considerate that they will help their females raise puppies by playing with them or even guarding them during the female's temporary absences. Males tend also

The Hairless Crested is prone to skin problems.

to be calmer than females and less dependent on their owners. If a person must work long hours, a male Chinese Crested could be a better option. However, neither male nor female Chinese Cresteds will be happy in such a situation.

Although neither sex likes to be forced to accept the things they dislike, females tend to hold a grudge for longer periods than males, and such acts as a forceful nail clipping may result in a resentful pet giving its owner the silent treatment.

Females also tend to be more emotional and therefore can be harder to housebreak. The removal of the ovaries is the only foolproof method of preventing unwanted pregnancies, but it will not affect female behavior, other than making them act in more masculine ways.

Not every hairless dog is a Chinese Crested.

Showing dogs can be expensive and requires a good handler and a great dog.

Thus, a spayed female may begin to raise her leg to mark territory or become more protective of her owner.

Show Prospect or Pet?

Many people are drawn to the idea of having a show-quality dog. Some individuals are genuinely interested in the competition and know what they are looking for by studying the Standard, and some are at the novice stage and unsure about the qualities a show dog must possess. In addition, a whole group of people just want a show-quality dog for a pet.

If a person is a novice, he or she should, before actually purchasing a dog, study the breed and then attend shows to watch the win-

ning dogs to understand the type and qualities that breeders present in the ring as their ideal representation of the Standard. Then the novice should study the pedigree of the winning dogs. (These can be obtained at various web sites or provided by the AKC.)

When choosing a prospective show dog, people should base their choices on the following points: adherence to the Standard, pedigree, temperament, health, and soundness. All issues must be considered equally important. A healthy dog may become someone's cherished pet, but not necessarily a show dog. Similarly, the best-bred dog, with impeccable confirmation, may make a poor show prospect if he lacks proper attitude or a talent for self-presentation.

If it were necessary to point to one single characteristic of the Chinese Crested dog as most important, it would be the type. To be a Chinese Crested dog, an animal must look like one. A novice should study photos of winning dogs to learn which type is correct.

A show prospect also has to have a flowing movement that commands attention and has to act self-assured. Side-winding, a hackneyed gait, a wobbly topline, flat shoulders, wide rears, or cow hocks and narrow fronts are all faults and will prevent the dog from quickly winning, and even the best hired handler may not be able to help.

The novice should not expect to be able to acquire the best-quality dog right at the start. Because good-quality Chinese Cresteds are rare and highly desired, many breeders refuse to sell their best dogs to people lacking show experience, thinking it would be a "waste" of a good dog. Of course, money talks, but the price may be well above the financial ability of the average person. In many cases, the breeder's hesitancy to give away a good dog to a novice can be justified, as most beginners cannot bring the dog to the same heights of popularity as an experienced exhibitor.

Financial Considerations

Another important thing to point out here is that not many novices realize how expensive showing dogs can be. Professional handlers charge money for training, boarding, and showing dogs, and often require that the owner advertise the winnings in canine magazines that promote the dog and his handler. After all, a professional handler's title comes only after many years of training experience and many successful performances in the show ring. People may want to show their own dogs. However, the Chinese Crested breed is not easy for beginners, and the Hairless variety, which seems more prone to mood changes, requires patience in addition to experience. With some effort, an amateur owner may eventually become as good as any professional handler, but success may not be seen for quite a while.

Reputable breeders of Chinese Crested dogs who sincerely want to better the breed, exemplified by the quality of their dogs, should be willing to fully cooperate with novices in making them aware of any defects and health problems they may have encountered in their line. In a word, they should be willing to become novices' mentors.

Although high-quality Hairless dogs are often beyond the financial means of a novice because of their high prices, Powderpuffs are not, and often there are quite a few to choose from and at very reasonable prices. The breeder will also be more inclined to sell an exceptional-quality Powderpuff to a novice than the same-quality Hairless.

It takes time, money, and experience to show a Chinese Crested.

The Powderpuff coat should be of proper volume, long, and silky. The ears should be erect and preferably strong enough to support the long hair fringes. Missing teeth in the Hairless are allowable, but they are considered a major fault in the Powderpuff. When selecting a puppy, choose the one with the best confirmation, the best set of ears, and the silkiest and most voluminous coat. Hair that is too thin will produce a coat that will mat easily, whereas a coat that is too short or frizzy will create an imbalanced silhouette.

The Chinese Crested, whether a pet or a show prospect, should not be chosen on the basis of looks alone, color, or size (for example, some people want only a teacup). Temperament, health, and soundness must be considered, too. A beautiful but sickly, mean-spirited, or poorly socialized puppy is not a joy to have around, whereas a dog that is perhaps less attractive but sound and with a sweet temperament will make a cherished and trusted friend for life.

Generally speaking, pets can be divided into dogs that have some faults, which prevent them from taking part in confirmation events, and dogs that are considered show quality but are sold as pets. Ideally, all pets should be good enough to compete at shows, and some substandard dogs may or may not be suitable for pets. Dogs with poor skin condition, extreme over- or underbite, and various genetic and congenital health disorders should be offered for adoption to people familiar with the special needs of Chinese Crested dogs.

When buying your Hairless puppy, you must seriously consider his skin condition. If you have

Most rescue dogs make exceptionally affectionate and very loyal pets. Getting a rescue dog over a puppy gives your dog a new lease on life he otherwise would not have.

no time for daily or even weekly baths, you should seek a dog with the best skin possible. If you are concerned about housebreaking (and the Hairless Chinese Crested can be particularly hard to train), you should opt for the Powderpuff or an older dog already broken in by the breeder.

A caring buyer should never insist on taking home a six-week-old puppy. Chinese Crested puppies are rarely mature enough to go to a new home at that young age, and still require a mother's care.

At the fourth month of age, the teeth may still not be fully developed, and it may be hard to judge the final condition of a bite. Because the upper jaw grows faster than the lower, any overbite at this age should, as a rule, be looked upon with suspicion. A mild underbite is nor-

mal, however, and often by the time a puppy gets permanent teeth, the bite improves enough to become a level or scissor type.

A well-bred Chinese Crested dog should be friendly with people and other animals and have clean habits. There is nothing more unpleasant than a dog that cannot be house-trained or soils its crate, a yapping dog, or one that snaps at any opportunity. A dog that cannot be handled because of shyness is a poor prospect as a family pet. An aggressive dog should immediately be rejected. Although it is possible on occasion to modify aggressive behaviors with special therapy, dogs with a problem temperament should be handled only by individuals with adequate experience and knowledge of canine psychology.

Rescue and Adoption

There are many reasons why Chinese Cresteds end up in rescue programs or shelters. An owner's death, illness, hospitalization, job loss, and financial instability are common causes, in addition to the simple fact that once cherished pets may have outlived their usefulness. Many Chinese Cresteds are also removed from abusive homes, and unfortunately, animal cruelty and neglect knows no bounds.

It must also be said that some breeders add to the problem of unwanted pets by refusing to accept "returns," forcing the owners to turn a dog over to a local pound or shelter. Sometimes the dogs are left on the sidewalk or the highway to fend for themselves, and if they are lucky, they are found by animal welfare author-

A Chinese Crested puppy needs lots of love and care.

ities and sent to the pound where rescue groups pick them up.

Crest Care is a Chinese Crested rescue organization that retrieves abandoned dogs from local pounds and shelters to rehabilitate and find new adoptive homes for them. For information on how to sponsor or adopt a Chinese Crested dog, contact Crest Care at *www.crest-care.com.*

Chinese Cresteds who have lost their once-happy homes because of various unhappy circumstances are the ones that suffer the most from missing their owners. If you are adopting a Chinese Crested from such a situation, you will need to be patient and allow your dog time to grieve and overcome his sorrow.

Dogs that were abused or neglected may have a psychological barrier that will not allow them to interact easily with their adoptive parents. They need to be treated with understanding and kindness to be able to forget their bad past experiences and to learn once again how to trust and have confidence in humans.

Prevent Abuse Before It Starts

Studies in psychology, sociology, and criminology during the last 30 years have demonstrated a definite link between violent criminals and animal abuse. Anthropologist Margaret Mead once wrote: "One of the most dangerous things that can happen to a child is to kill or torture an animal and get away with it."

One should never allow children to be cruel to animals or to watch animal abuse without explaining its wrongness. This is particularly true in relation to Chinese Crested dogs, which may seem to a child more like funny toys than living creatures, and are thus often subject to insensitive treatment.

Occasionally, older Chinese Crested dogs, often retired champions and brood bitches, are offered for adoption for a small fee by breeders who wish to place them in a home where they can spend the latter part of their lives with a loving family and away from the stress of kennel life. Many of them are of a superior quality, representing the breeder's best. However, because the dogs are usually of advanced age, it is always advisable to check the health of a prospective adoptee to make a fully informed decision, as the medical expenses can be too much for even the most devoted Crested lover.

Most rescues make exceptionally affectionate and loyal pets.

HOW TO FIND A REPUTABLE BREEDER

Finding a trustworthy breeder may take more than one visit or phone call. It may even require travel. Good breeders are hard to find, and when they are found, they usually have long waiting lists. However, wanting the best requires patience.

Recognizing a Reputable Breeder

Finding a reputable Chinese Crested breeder can be a difficult task since all breeders present themselves as such. However, there are certain signs by which it may be possible to recognize whether a breeder's claim is true or false. The main difference between reputable breeders and backyard breeders lies in their goals. A backyard breeder's interest in breeding dogs is to make profit, whereas the reputable breeder's motivation is to perfect the breed.

Backyard breeders usually try to get rid of the puppies as soon the dam stops cleaning after them, which usually happens around five

Finding the right breeder is just as important as finding the right dog.

weeks. They want to assume as little responsibility for the puppies' futures as possible, so guarantees are nonexistent or inadequate. Typically, puppies are advertised for sale before they are born, and health tests are not perfomed after birth. Buyers are usually invited to a garage or a kitchen, or sometimes only to the front of a gas station, where, after a few polite remarks, cash is exchanged for puppies, and from that moment on, owners and dogs are on their own. If a puppy gets sick the next day, or is found full of worms or suffering a defect, there is rarely any possibility for a refund or an exchange past the customary 24 hours and maximum three days. So when it comes to taking legal action against such a breeder, where is the contract to make a claim? As a rule, backyard breeders avoid any contracts or written agreements that may incriminate them or hold them to their word. Some backyard breeders are able occasionally to obtain their breeding stock from show breeders, usually under the false pretense that they want to show and promote the breed; however, once they start breeding, they soon lower the quality by indiscriminate breeding or through ignorance.

Which of these two advertisements describes a reputable breeder?

This:

> Adorable, ready-to-go 5-week-old Chinese Crested pups for sale, champion lines, raised underfoot. $500 cash only on first-come basis. Hurry! 1-800-000-0000

Or this?

> 12-week-old Chinese Crested puppies, pet or show prospects, for sale to approved homes. Pets sold with a spay/neuter contract only. References and written agreement required. Lifetime breeder's support. 1-888-000-0000

In contrast, reputable breeders can be recognized by their adherence to the Chinese Crested Standard and by the care and attention they give their dogs. They usually do not breed more than two breeds of dogs. Anyone who breeds multiple varieties of dogs cannot possibly give enough attention to them and should be avoided.

Reputable breeders strive to eliminate defects in their lines by doing health tests on their dogs. Breeding better dogs is a matter of pride to them and often a lifetime goal. Although getting a puppy from such a breeder may involve an extra expense, such as shipping from another state or traveling in person to get the dog, or even a higher price, the dog will not only be of better quality, but will also come with the

Better to be too careful than sorry! Reputable breeders and clever puppy buyers insist on contracts!

breeder's lifetime support. In addition, reputable breeders will have plenty of easily available references supporting their claims to respectability, which buyers should check carefully before paying a deposit or signing a contract.

Similarly, reputable breeders always check their buyers' references to make sure they are responsible people and can be entrusted with a dog. A reputable breeder will also insist on a contract, which should be written with the dog's welfare in mind and provide legal protection for the owner, not just shelter the breeder from liabilities. A properly written legal contract motivates the buyer and the seller to take responsibility for the sale in case things go wrong.

Strings Attached

Some strings, or extra conditions, should be expected, but they are mainly for the protection of the breed and the dog. In the case of a pet, the main requirement is that your dog be spayed or neutered. The other conditions are that the dog will be given loving care and veterinary assistance in case of illness. The pet contract should also describe the penalties in case the buyer or breeder decides to break the agreement.

Show-dog contracts are typically more stringent, often requiring some co-ownership and that buyers hire handlers in case their handling skills are inadequate. Other conditions could have to do with advertising the dog and even sharing the first litter with the breeder. Of course, if buyers cannot accept these conditions, they can always find easier breeders; however,

*A backyard breeder's interest in breeding
dogs is to make a profit, while the reputable
breeder's motivation is to perfect the breed.*

as a rule, the better the dogs that particular breeders offer for sale and the larger the number of champions to their credit, the higher the price and the more strings attached. In addition, many top breeders require that a show-quality bitch or male be bred only to a certain line approved by them. This provision is not a result of the breeders' vanity, but rather of their knowledge of the breed and the gene pool. After all, great Chinese Cresteds are not born every day, and breeders must work very hard and for many years to achieve some measure of success, so it is only natural that they would want to protect their lines from being ruined by reckless or ignorant breeding decisions.

Reputable breeders will also offer buyers lifetime support and demand that the Cresteds be returned to them if for any reason owners or their immediate families can no longer take good care of the dogs. They will provide buyers with health records and plenty of instructions. They will also not hide any defects in their lines (all have some!) and will describe honestly your puppy's temperament, guaranteeing her suitability as a family pet or her show potential.

Ideally, you should visit the breeder before finalizing the purchase. However, it may not be possible or even practical, since a majority of Chinese Crested dogs today are bought on the Internet and shipped sight unseen, merely based on a photo and the breeder's word. Establishing trust between the breeder and the buyer is, therefore, the most important ingredient for success. To begin, you should ask the breeder the following questions:

1. Will the breeder's veterinarian check the puppy before shipping?

2. Has the puppy received any vaccinations or other treatments, and if so, which ones?

3. Is the puppy microchipped or tattooed?

4. In case the dog has to be returned, who will pay the cost of the exchange? Will the refund be available, and under what conditions? How soon will a replacement be available? (A reasonable time is six months.)

5. What kind of health tests has the breeder done to guarantee the puppy's health?

6. Should a puppy be found to suffer from a genetic defect requiring emergency surgery, who will be liable for the expenses?

7. If the puppy (or an adult dog) is sold as a show prospect, how long will the co-ownership last and what are the options for the buyer if the dog is discovered to be sterile?

8. If it is a male puppy, are both testicles normal and fully descended?

9. Can the dog be returned if it is no longer wanted?

10. Has the puppy been socialized appropriately for its age, and is the puppy familiar with small children?

If you are comfortable with the provided answers and have checked the breeder's references to your satisfaction, the next thing is to try to determine how the puppy will look at maturity. As a rule of thumb, doubling the height of a six-week-old puppy can roughly describe her size at maturity. Thus, if a puppy is 6 inches (15 cm) tall at the shoulder at six weeks, she most likely will grow to be 12 inches (30 cm). The puppy's weight is less predictable, although some breeders believe that a weight at three months multiplied by two, plus or minus a pound, can predict the weight of an adult dog. However, this is not always true. Some puppies stay very small for many months, only to shoot up at six or nine months, and many larger puppies stop growing at four months. Although there is a large market for the teacup-size Chinese Cresteds, particularly the Hairless ones, they are very rare and often subject to hypoglycemia or heart problems. In spite of claims to the contrary, tiny Chinese Crested teacups do exist, but because of their fragility, taking care of them requires a lifelong responsibility on the part of the owner. They can also be more expensive because of their rareness and the extra effort necessary in raising them. If thinking about buying a tiny dog for breeding, a person must be aware that very small male dogs are as a rule sterile, and tiny bitches are too delicate to be safely whelped. Nearly all tiny dogs that reach adulthood are born from regular-size parents. Nature obviously takes care that such weaklings do not propagate.

Finally, the price. Good-quality Chinese Cresteds, whether pets or show prospects, are not cheap. Pet quality Chinese Crested Hairless dogs typically start at $750 and show quality at $1,000, going up to $3,000 for the most outstanding prospects. The Powderpuffs may cost less, but much depends on demand, which is usually dictated by fashion. Of course, price is not always indicative of quality; however, Chinese Crested dogs are very expensive to breed. In addition, their litters are small, often consisting of one puppy only. In fact, most reputable breeders hardly make any profit from the sale, unlike many backyard breeders, who keep their expenses to a minimum.

Backyard Breeders and Puppy Mills

Puppy mills are breeding factories where dogs are kept like chickens in overcrowded, filthy conditions. Puppy mills have many breeds of dogs—among them, unfortunately, the Chinese Crested. Inside these establishments, dogs are treated as puppy-producing machines, being bred time after time until their bodies give out. Puppies are sold at six weeks, per pound, to the dog brokers arriving on a regular basis. The "merchandise" is later loaded into huge trucks and shipped to unsuspecting buyers. Buyer beware!

Written Contracts or Verbal Agreements

Verbal or written agreements? Well, a verbal agreement is as good as the word of the person who speaks it, so the answer here is rather obvious. Only written and signed contracts can assure buyers that they have legal recourse if

Presence of the lethal gene explains why it is impossible to produce only Hairless offspring and breed out the coated variety.

things do not go as anticipated. A good contract must contain a full description of the dog or puppy, the registration numbers of the parents and the litter, and, if the purchase requires shipping, a microchip or tattoo information to include a photo for identification purposes. The contract should also include detailed conditions for obtaining registration papers. Some breeders will sell pets only without registration papers but will provide a pedigree; some will provide only a limited registration that does not permit registration of the offspring from the dog in question, thus enforcing the spay/neuter condition; and other breeders will provide registration papers only upon proof of spay/neuter surgery by a licensed veterinarian.

A list of Chinese Crested breeders can be obtained from the American Kennel Club, the

**Ethical Chinese Crested breeders
do not ship puppies younger than
ten weeks of age.**

The coat of the Powderpuff variety features a soft double coat over the entire body.

American Chinese Crested Club (national), and local clubs. Another good source is *Dog Fancy* magazine, breeders' web sites, and search engines. It must be remembered, however, that it is not important where breeders advertise, but whether they can support their claims to reputability.

Shipping

Shipping the Crested is less complicated than it sounds. Most Chinese Crested puppies travel well and arrive in good condition. However, they should never be shipped before ten weeks of age, particularly the Hairless Cresteds, which are prone to dehydration. It is usually up to the breeder to make a reservation with the airline and secure all the necessary documentation to make sure your puppy arrives safely. Once the puppy is on her way, the owner can monitor her whereabouts by calling the airline or checking

Many states have laws that protect buyers from sick or defective puppies bought from a pet store or breeder.

online. The cost of shipping is usually the buyer's responsibility, on top of the puppy's price. The buyer typically picks up the dog in a cargo office or at the baggage counter. Most airlines take good care of the animals in cargo, and accidents are very rare. However, to be on the safe side, it is always a good idea to pay an extra fee for insurance.

You should bring to the airport a warm blanket, a couple of towels, fresh water, a little snack, and, for an older dog, a lead. If the trip was long, the puppy may arrive soiled or wet. For sure, she will be thirsty, hungry, and tired. To prevent any possibility of escape, the kennel should not be opened until you and the dog are in a secure place, perhaps inside a car. There, the puppy can be taken out from her kennel, cleaned, and offered some water. Because the plane trip was without a doubt a major event in the dog's life, it is important to comfort the dog. Now is the best time to make the dog feel loved and wanted, and to present oneself as a new parent and friend for life. Hugging and kissing does wonders, and so does a tasty little snack. A piece of barbecued chicken can be an icebreaker!

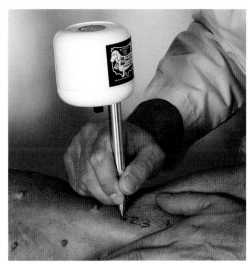

Your dog's identification, whether by tattoo, tags, or microchip, or a combination of the three, should be confirmed upon arrival at the airport.

A written agreement can give you some assurance of your puppy's quality, and gives you legal recourse if needed.

LOVING THE CHINESE CRESTED

Here comes the Chinese Crested! Sensitive, affectionate, capricious, moody, and self-indulgent, the Chinese Crested dog requires not only an emotional commitment, but also a substantial financial one. In return, he will offer his owner undying devotion and loyalty.

Home, Sweet Home . . .

Home at last! The first thing to do is to let the puppy out to the yard to his "wee-wee pad" place. Once the dog finishes with his needs, you should offer your puppy water and food. If the puppy refuses to eat (this is normal), he may be too excited or still unsure of the new situation. Nevertheless, the dog should be coerced to drink some water to prevent possible dehydration.

If the puppy is not too tired, you can take him on a house tour. The same day or the next, you should do a simple health check to see if the dog suffers from any health problems and make notes to discuss them with the breeder and the veterinarian.

More sensitive Cresteds may need more time to recuperate from the shock of travel and a

Powderpuff or Hairless, the Chinese Crested can make a great pet.

change of home. You should allow at least three or four days for adjustment, if not longer.

Although it is understandable that the love-stricken owners may wish to share a bed with their new pet or let him just live on a couch, the dog will still need a secure place of his own, a safe little haven that includes all daily used items. Laundry rooms, closets, or bathrooms are the wrong places to keep a dog, particularly one such as the Chinese Crested.

The best and proven solution for a new owner is a plastic playpen, 4 by 6 feet (1.2 by 1.8 m) or better yet, 6 by 6 feet (1.8 by 1.8 m), and about 3 or 4 feet (1–1.2 m) high. This pen, placed away from the main traffic and drafts, should be set in one of the rooms, perhaps a kitchen, as this is where most of the interesting action takes place. This "Chinese Crested kingdom" should be furnished with everything that the pet may need, such as food and water bowls, a plush bed, toys, a wee-wee pad, and

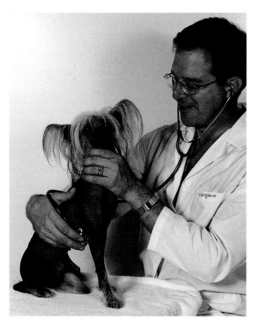

The day after arrival, a competent veterinarian should check the new Crested puppy to see if he suffers from any health problems.

CHECKLIST

New Arrival Check-up

1. Are the dog's eyes clean, free of discharge and redness?
2. Are both eyes the same size?
3. Is the skin clean and healthy looking?
4. Is the dog dehydrated? To test this, pick up a fold of skin and release it quickly. If a dog is dehydrated, the skin will take some time returning to its place.
5. Are the dog's gums pink or white? White gums can signify shock or anemia.
6. Does the dog have retained puppy teeth? Retained puppy teeth must be pulled out by a veterinarian.
7. Are the dog's ears clean?
8. Do both ears have open ear canals? Dogs with missing ear canals are deaf.
9. Is the dog coughing or does he have a fever?
10. Does the dog have diarrhea or is he urinating a lot?
11. Is the dog's stool firm, free of worms or blood?
12. Is the dog underweight or potbellied?
13. Is the dog acting normal? Prolonged lethargy is a sign of sickness.
14. Is the dog friendly and outgoing or shy?
15. Is the dog's fontanel closed or open?

perhaps a padded kennel to hide and sleep in. While giving the pet a sense of privacy, such an arrangement also prevents destructive behavior and teaches clean habits. It is also particularly useful in a situation when the pet's new parents are not at home. In addition, giving a puppy his own space means he will not be a nuisance to visiting guests or whenever the owner wishes to be alone.

While the pen can be a great training tool, it should never become a prison for your pet. Your dog will still need to be socialized and should physically interact with you and other members of your household, as well as with guests who may occasionally come to visit. Lack of physical contact can change any nice dog into a morose, unhappy pet. You should keep your Crested in the pen only when the situation warrants it, or if you have to confine him for training, medical, or security reasons.

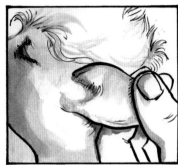

One dog with an open ear canal (left), and one with a closed ear canal (right).

Once the puppy is fully trained, he should have complete access to the house, particularly the living room or family room, wherever he can mingle with the family and experience a feeling of belonging. This will make him a better pet, more devoted to you, better socialized, and less emotionally insecure.

Open Fontanel

Some Chinese Crested puppies, in particular the Hairless ones, may still have an open fontanel when they go to their new homes. The fontanel is a soft spot at the top of a puppy's skull where all the skull plates join. At birth, the bony plates of the skull are separated, but as the puppy grows, they gradually fuse together. In most cases, the fontanel closes by eight weeks of age. However, occasionally the fontanel never closes, leaving a soft, very sensitive spot. Any blow can cause severe brain damage, hydrocephalus, or even death. If the Crested shows an open fontanel, and it looks swollen, it may indicate fluid buildup underneath the skull or a hydrocephalic brain. Otherwise, if the puppy appears healthy and normal in all other respects, there may be no cause for concern. However, the defect must be considered congenital and affected dogs should be excluded from breeding.

Closed Ear Canals

Another important defect seen among the Chinese Cresteds is a closed ear canal, which affects mostly the Hairless variety. The ear, often smaller and of unusual shape, lacks an opening or a canal leading to the inner ear. Chinese Cresteds with missing ear canals are either completely deaf or can hear only high-pitched sounds. The defect is congenital, and surgeries to open the ear are usually unsuccessful.

Occasionally, Chinese Crested Hairless dogs have closed ear canals.

Chinese Cresteds love children, but do not like to be harassed by them.

Dry Eye

Dry eye is a common disorder among Chinese Cresteds. Dry eye is called KCS or Keratoconjunctivitis Sicca. It occurs when a dog doesn't make enough tears to keep the eyes lubricated. The symptoms of KCS are lack of tears, bulging and/or red eye, and sticky discharge. Once dry eye develops, most pets will need medication for the remainder of their lives. Occasionally, it is possible to correct the problem with surgery; otherwise the dog must be treated with medication on a daily basis. The medication does not cure the problem; it only helps to control it. In most Cresteds, this condition can be caused by a problem in the immune system, an untreated eye infection, a virus, such as distemper, or physical injury to the eye.

Introducing Children and Other Pets

Before your new Crested pet is introduced to other pets or small children, make sure the dog

CHECKLIST

Chinese Crested Paraphernalia

The paraphernalia list for Chinese Cresteds should consist of everyday items for the dog's care, including grooming and conditioning supplies.

1. Plastic X-pen
2. Whitening shampoo to remove stains from the furnishings or coat
3. Shampoo and conditioner for regular use
4. First aid supplies
5. Anti-acne medication and scrubs
6. Conditioning skin oil or cream
7. Brush, slicker, and comb
8. Oxy pads
9. Nail clipper
10. Braun shaver to remove hair stubs from the hairy Hairless Crested
11. Hair trimmer, such as Wahl's Peanut model
12. A lead, preferably a soft "kindness" type
13. Diapers for a boy dog and panties for a girl dog
14. Wee-wee pads
15. Toys
16. Pet carrier or bag
17. T-shirts, sweat suit, sweaters
18. Pooper scooper
19. Toothbrush and doggy toothpaste
20. Sunscreen lotion

is relaxed and in a friendly mood. Small children should be asked to be gentle with the dog, especially if he is a small puppy. Some Cresteds

Chinese Cresteds get easily bored and dislike being left alone at home.

really dislike being grabbed from behind, particularly pulling by the tail. It is better to wait until the dog approaches the children first. If the dog becomes uneasy, it may be better to keep him away until he settles down. Owners with other dogs should expect that they, as first-comers, might react negatively to a new family member competing for the attention of the "parent." However, if they are offered extra hugs and are verbally reassured of the owner's love, they may accept the situation without much fuss. Still, the first meeting must be fully supervised with nothing left to chance, especially if the "other" dog is much larger or is of

a protective breed, such as a Mastiff. If the pets show hostility to each other, they should be separated and introduced again the next day. If there is no change in their attitudes, a routine meeting should be established until the hostility ceases. Eventually, the barrier will be broken and friendship will evolve.

The average Chinese Crested dog is very fond of cats and birds. Of course, you should supervise any interaction with birds. Large birds, particularly parrots, can seriously injure or kill the Chinese Crested. With cats, the main problem is your puppy's attraction to the litter box, which should be permanently placed beyond its reach.

The Hairless is harder to train and housebreak than the Powderpuff.

ual. But if the meeting went well, you should request recent references from the sitter's other clients to make sure that you can entrust your beloved pet to his/her care. After all, you will be leaving your dog in the care of a total stranger.

To avoid any misunderstandings, you should also ask the pet sitter the following questions:

1. "How often will you be letting the dog out or taking him for a walk?"

2. "Are you familiar with emergency procedures in case the dog gets hurt or becomes ill?"

3. "If the dog needs to be taken to the hospital, what would be the extra charge?"

After you decide on a sitter, remember to supply him/her with your contact information and your veterinarian's phone number in case a problem arises. In addition, you will need to instruct him/her on the diet needs of your dog, his feeding schedule, and toilet routine. Considering how difficult it is to housetrain a Crested, the feeding and toilet routine is particularly important and should not be changed unless absolutely necessary.

Day Care or a Pet Sitter?

If you work long hours, you should decide if your Chinese Crested will be attending a day care center during your absence or if it would be better to hire a pet sitter. If you have other pets, hiring a sitter may be more practical. On the other hand, a pet care center will provide your pet with socialization and entertainment. Hiring a pet sitter often works very well, too, because the dog can enjoy daily walks and interaction with other humans, instead of passively waiting and sulking alone about his mom or dad.

Before hiring a pet sitter, you should arrange a meeting between your pet and the pet sitter to see if she/he and the dog get along. If your dog does not like the sitter, reacts aggressively, or runs away, you should not hire that individ-

Sharing the Bed with the Chinese Crested

Chinese Crested dogs would make great hot water bottles if they wanted to sleep at the foot of the bed, but they prefer their owners' heads! Usually they sleep well through the night, at the same time keeping very alert. In this respect, they make great watchdogs. Nevertheless, many Crested pets also break their legs by jumping from a bed, so it would be a good idea to install a ramp or pet stairs, so the dog could use them instead of having to jump down. Young puppies should wear a panty with a diaper inside to avoid soiling the sheets.

Boarding the Chinese Crested

Sometimes it may be necessary to send your Chinese Crested to a boarding kennel. All boarding facilities require that the dogs have an up-to-date record of shots and a rabies certificate. In addition, it would be wise also to have the dog inoculated against kennel cough, leptospirosis, and giardia. Most Cresteds intensely dislike being boarded, so to ease your dog's anguish, bring some of his favorite toys to the kennel and ask the manager to feed him the same food he gets at home, or provide the kennel with some of the same food.

Traveling with the Chinese Crested

Chinese Cresteds make great travel companions, but if they are not used to automobile trips, they can get carsick. One of the best preventive remedies is ginger, which can be given either as tea, in capsules, or as a sublingual spray (the best!) before the trip. The dosage should be the same as for a small child. Since Chinese Cresteds are known to have sensitive stomachs, it is better to bring some bottled water from home or buy spring or purified water for a trip.

If the trip is going to be long, the Chinese Crested travel pack should include all supplies that the dog uses at home and toys to keep him occupied. A rubber ball or a Frisbee to play "throw and bring back" games will provide you and your dog with quality time together. In addition, taking an exercise pen allows the

owner to stop and let the dog rest, eat, and attend to his toilet needs.

Many hotels and motels allow dogs for an extra charge. The most popular are Travel Lodge, Western Motel, Motel 6, and Holiday Inn, but call ahead to make sure.

To make traveling safer, the Crested pet should be placed in either a kennel or a car booster seat that attaches to the passenger seat and allows the dog to look out the window and enjoy the view. A pet carrier is another "must" to have, especially for a young puppy.

If going to the beach or on a boat, it is a good idea to provide the dog with a life jacket. They come in many colors and are provided with a handle that allows you to grab the dog in case of emergency.

If you plan to travel with your Crested by plane, you should be aware that unless the kennel fits under the seat, the dog will have to be shipped as cargo. Only a puppy small enough to fit into a carry-on bag can accompany you on board.

Prior to starting your trip, you will need to make reservations for your pet and find out what may be required of the place you are going to visit. In addition, you may have to show a valid shipping certificate and proof of an updated rabies vaccine.

Sherpa bags specifically made for small animals are an excellent choice to use for a plane trip. However, the bag should be large enough so your pet can turn around, stand up, or sit down comfortably. Do not forget to take with you some wee-wee pads in case the puppy gets sick or needs to relieve himself. You can go to the bathroom on board to attend to the needs of your puppy, but you should also be prepared to clean up after him.

Bon Voyage!

FEEDING THE CHINESE CRESTED

The Chinese Crested is an omnivorous creature and will thrive on a wholesome diet of meats, fruits, and vegetables.

Home Diet, Commercial Food, or BARF

Chinese Crested dogs enjoy eating a variety of foods, including fruits, nuts, and vegetables. In fact, peanut butter sandwiches are a favorite snack for many. In that sense, they are easy to feed. However, food allergies are common to the Chinese Crested, and for this reason not every diet is suitable for them. Also, poor-quality food, whether dry commercial or homemade, can cause serious skin problems.

Organic commercial food formulas usually provide the most nutritious ingredients necessary for maintaining a healthy Chinese Crested dog. Some of the best digestible dog foods for Chinese Cresteds are Innova, California Natural,

The Chinese Crested puppy should eat at least four meals a day.

and Solid Gold. Still, even the best commercial food will need to be supplemented with fruit and green vegetables so your pet will have a complete diet. In addition, lack of fiber, which is derived from raw fruit and vegetables, will cause the Chinese Crested to eat grass.

Strawberries, apples with their cores removed, sweet peas, broccoli, and carrots seem to be favorite snacks for many Cresteds, as is a lettuce salad with vinaigrette or Italian dressing.

For Chinese Cresteds suffering from food allergies or skin problems, a home diet or BARF may be more beneficial than commercial formulas.

A home diet is made with cooked ingredients. Often the main meal consists of rice and meat, or meat and mashed potatoes. The meat is usually either a whole chicken cooked in a steam cooker together with the bones, or ground beef. In addition, the dog is fed an unlimited supply of commercial dry-food formula.

Chinese Crested dogs enjoy eating a variety of foods, including fruits, nuts, and vegetables.

The term *BARF* stands for "bones and raw food." The BARF diet advocates feeding raw, meaty bones, vegetables, and fruit in an attempt to imitate a natural diet a dog would eat in the wild. Raw meaty bones comprise chicken necks, backs, thighs, and rib cages, ox tails, and pigs' feet. Organ meats and occasionally fish with the bones removed should be used as well. Another source of protein is raw eggs together with their shells ground finely in a blender.

Because Chinese Crested dogs have weak, easily breakable teeth, large or hard bones need to be ground in a food processor.

Raw vegetables include broccoli, carrots, celery, peas, and green beans. Adding a pinch of kelp powder to a meal will supply many rare minerals, including iodine, which is necessary for maintaining a healthy thyroid. Some BARF diets allow for cooked brown rice, grits, or oatmeal.

Regardless of which diet you decide to choose—a commercial dry food, home cooking, or a strict BARF—the complete Chinese Crested menu must incorporate raw vegetables and fruits. An adult Chinese Crested should have three meals a day, and puppies at least four or more.

Here is an example of a typical adult daily menu for a standard-size Chinese Crested dog. Older dogs should have slightly smaller portions.

Morning:

¼ cup (57 g) dry food mixed with 1 Tbs. (14 g) yogurt

¼ pound (125 g) raw ground beef (fat content 25 percent or more) with 1 tsp (4.7 g) finely chopped parsley

1 small sliced raw carrot or ⅓ cup (76 g) of raw green beans

Noon:

1 Tbs. (14 g) cottage cheese with ½ tsp. (2 mL) flax-seed oil

½ apple with core removed

1 hard-boiled egg

Evening:

¼ cup (57 g) dry food

¼ cup lettuce with dressing made of apple-cider vinegar and olive oil

Raw beef liver, chicken, or lamb can be substituted for ground beef; strawberries, pears, oranges, or bananas for apples; carrots, cauliflower, broccoli, green peas, green peppers, or cabbage for green beans; a sardine for an egg; tofu for cottage cheese; and pumpkin oil for flax-seed oil. Experiment with various foods to find which ones your Crested pet enjoys the most. Some Cresteds will not touch broccoli but enjoy green pepper, whereas others will eat only fruit and refuse cottage cheese. If you decide on a strict BARF diet, the rule of thumb is to feed the Crested 85 percent meat or meat products, including ground bones, 10 percent raw green vegetables, and 5 percent fruit.

It is important to remember that the food, particularly if raw, must always be fresh, as food-borne pathogens, such as clostridium perfringens, can make your Crested very sick or even kill her if left untreated. In addition, the dog's food bowl and feeding area must be very clean and regularly disinfected to prevent contamination. Symptoms of food poisoning are fecal mucus, fresh blood in the stool, scant stools, and increased frequency of defecation. Vomiting may or may not be present.

Finicky Eaters

The majority of finicky eaters are often spoiled brats, but it is important to distinguish between the capricious pet and a sick one. If the change in eating habits is abrupt, and your pet previously was never too meticulous about her food, a sudden loss of appetite could signal an illness requiring veterinarian intervention.

Otherwise, the fault often lies in allowing the dog to feast on kitchen leftovers. To change this bad habit, you need to introduce some discipline. The simplest solution is to start feeding on schedule. Meals should be offered twice (if a finicky eater) or, in the case of a puppy, three times a day, and at the same exact hour, allowing the dog about 15 minutes to eat. What is not eaten during that time should be removed until the next scheduled meal. To increase your pet's appetite, the food can be spiced with some smelly cheese such as a Parmesan or blue cheese. A few bacon bits will also do the trick. A healthy Chinese Crested pet will not refuse food when hungry, unless she is too afraid or nervous. In such a situation, the dog needs to be allowed to have her meal in solitude.

Overweight or Obese Chinese Crested

Obesity is never normal in a dog, particularly one as active as the Chinese Crested. Therefore, if

Paw-Licking Liver Cookies

1 cup (226 g) oatmeal
1½ cups (339 g) whole-wheat flour
¼ cup (60 mL) molasses
1 cup (226 g) mashed raw carrots
⅓ cup (58 g) chopped parsley
2 whole eggs
1½ lb. (730 g) chopped liver
1 Tbs. (15 mL) vegetable oil
2 Tbs. (28 g) of yogurt
2 slivers chopped garlic

Preheat oven to 350°F (180°C). Mix the ingredients well. Add water as needed. Drop on cookie sheet using a spoon. Bake 15–20 minutes or until golden brown. Makes approximately 40 small cookies.

Beef Bon-Bons

2 cups (453 g) whole-wheat flour
¼ cup (60 mL) olive or canola oil
¼ cup (60 mL) melted butter
1 beaten whole egg
6 Tbs. (100 mL) water
1 cup (226 g) fried ground beef with a
   chopped sliver of garlic

Preheat oven to 350°F (180°C). Mix flour, butter, egg, oil, and water. Add ground meat. Drop by spoon on a greased baking pan. Bake 20 to 25 minutes. Bon appetite!

a dog eats the same amount as always, yet is getting obese, a complete health checkup is necessary, since obesity could be caused by serious hormonal disorders. However, if the Crested's obesity is caused by a voracious appetite, then putting the dog on a diet should be enough to bring her back into shape. Raw green beans in particular have been found to quicken metabolism and should be fed daily. The obese Crested has to be fed on a strict schedule, and leftovers and snacks, particularly with a high fat content such as pig ears, should be removed from her menu. Daily exercise is a must!

Individual Preferences and Special Needs

Chinese Cresteds with chronic diseases such as heart problems, liver and gastrointestinal disorders, or kidney stones will need special diets. There are different diet formulas for different

problems, which need to be prepared on an individual basis by a canine nutritionist or a veterinarian. If your Crested suffers from simple diarrhea, she should abstain from solid food and be put on a liquid diet until the problem is resolved. A thin soup made from ¼ cup (57 g) of rice boiled in 3 cups (730 mL) water until the rice becomes mushy and can be put through a sieve is well tolerated by even the most sensitive Cresteds. If she refuses or is too weak to drink on her own, she should be fed with a large syringe or have the liquid spooned straight into her mouth. Chamomile tea can be offered instead of water. Older Cresteds suffering from loose stools will improve if their meals are sprinkled with a pinch of Metamucil or psyllium seeds. For chronic constipation, a flax-seed tea is suggested. A ¼ teaspoon (1 mL) of flax seeds soaked in a cup (250 mL) of boiling hot water and standing covered for 15 minutes will make a thick, gelatinous potion, which can be then mixed with either dry food or ground beef and fed to the dog in the evening to assure early-morning elimination.

A lactating bitch needs up to four times more calories per day than usual to produce enough milk for her puppies.

Cresteds suffering from diabetes require a high-fiber diet to help balance their sugar levels.

Lactating Bitches

A lactating bitch needs additional feedings. She needs up to four times more calories per day than usual so she can produce enough milk for her puppies. Extra cottage cheese, goat's milk, and egg yolks should be added to her regular diet to prevent low blood calcium or milk fever, also known as eclampsia, which is an acute, life-threatening condition. If you decide to use commercial calcium supplements, they must be in the proper ratio to phosphorus, about 1:1 (one part calcium to one part phosphorus).

The Aged Crested

Because they are less active, aged Cresteds should be fed less, but with high-quality food. It is also better to divide their portions into smaller meals. Chinese Crested Hairless dogs that have lost their teeth will have to be fed soft or moistened food.

Because heart disease is one of the main health concerns of aged dogs, flax-seed oil should be part of the daily menu of all geriatric Cresteds. Flax seed contains lecithin, which emulsifies fat and cholesterol, enhancing cardiovascular health and helping stabilize blood glucose levels. Flax seed also contains lignans that have antiviral, antibacterial, antifungal, and anticancer properties. Oil made from flax seed is the world's richest source of omega-3 fatty acids.

This cottage cheese and flax-seed-oil formula was adapted for the Chinese Crested dogs from a German recipe:

1 Tbs. (28 g) low fat cottage cheese
½ tsp. (2 mL) flax-seed oil
¼ tsp. (1 g) ground pumpkin seeds or sunflower seeds
½ tsp. (2 g) chopped parsley, a pinch of bacon seasoning, or ⅛ tsp. (.5 g) of bacon bits.

The meal should be served daily to the older Chinese Crested, and first thing in the morning before any other food.

Most older Cresteds maintain good appetite until the very end, although their stomachs become more sensitive with age. To prevent digestive upsets, the pet should be fed bland and soft foods. Vegetables can be slightly steamed to make them softer and easier to chew.

GROOMING AND BATHING

Grooming your Chinese Crested is not as simple as it may seem, especially the Hairless variety. Most Chinese Crested Hairless dogs, unless truly naked, need regular grooming and meticulous skin care to maintain healthy skin and look pleasing to the eye.

Basic Grooming Supplies

1. Clippers: Wahl clippers are the favorite of many Chinese Crested owners and show exhibitors. The Wahl Peanut and Oster's Mini Max are used for shaving faces and to remove excess hair from the hairy Crested. Wahl's Futura, Oster's Golden A5, and Andis Turbo A5 are heavy-duty clippers commonly used for cutting the Powderpuff's coat and doing a precise shaving of the hairy Hairless.

2. Snap-on clipper combs: These combs are used for trimming Powderpuff coats and to give them a longer clip.

3. Comb: The best combs have medium-spaced teeth and are made of Teflon or solid steel. The Greyhound style 7.5 is preferred for the Hairless Crested, the Evolution medium comb for the Powderpuff.

Correct grooming is the key to the Chinese Crested's successful show career.

4. Blades: Size #50 gives the closest cut. Size #40 is used on the body. Size #4 is for trimming down the Puff.

5. Brushes: Brushes should be of the best quality. The favorite of many exhibitors is the #1 All Systems. Smaller brushes are preferred for the Hairless Crested.

6. Slickers: These are used mainly on socks and plume to comb out mats and dirt. Only a mini-size is used: a little triangle slicker to brush the crest between the eyes and a square mini for the feet. Favorite slickers are Millers Forge and All Systems. Because the pins are very sharp, caution is advised to avoid injuring the pet.

7. Hair dryer: To blow-dry the coat and furnishings.

8. Nail clipper: For clipping the nails.

9. Nail file: To file out the sharp edges of newly clipped nails.

10. Scissors: To snip the hair from the ears or footpads.

11. Spray bottle filled with hair tonic or water: To use before brushing to prevent hair from breaking. In hot and dry climates, to prevent drying out, coats need to be misted daily, preferably with spring water.

12. Aftershave soothing cream or lotion: To be used on skin after shaving the Crested Hairless. The product should contain aloe vera, emu oil, or vitamin E.

13. Shampoo and conditioner: Many products can be used successfully on the Crested. Besides such general cleansing products as Orange Crème by Oster or Oatmeal Mella by Miracle Corporation, which can also be used on puppies, there are specific beauty formulas for show dogs. Products containing real silk are a well-guarded secret of many exhibitors. BioSilk, which is made for people, also works great for the Chinese Crested and can easily be found in most beauty supply shops. A similar product is Liquid Silk, a very small amount of which is rubbed between the palms before applying lightly to the coat or crest to give it a great sheen without a greasy look or buildup. Some owners also use mayonnaise as a conditioner to make coats soft and shiny.

14. Pet tub: For bathing the Crested. A variety of pet tubs are on the market as well as some alternatives (more on the subject on page 49).

Nails, Ears, and Teeth

Many Chinese Cresteds have dark nails, and the line separating the core from the hollow of the nail cannot always be seen. Because cutting too short will cause bleeding, it is better to leave nails a bit longer but trim them often. A nail file is used to smooth the edges. If the toenail is accidentally cut too short, applying some styptic powder to the affected nail and pushing it back with a cotton ball should stop the bleeding. Another method is to sprinkle a bit of powdered cayenne pepper on the bleeding nail. Cayenne pepper acts as a coagulating agent and is perfectly safe to use on little cuts.

The next important thing is ear cleaning. Cotton swabs soaked in a few drops of warmed olive or mineral oil can be used to dissolve earwax buildup. To remove dirt, swabs dipped in hydrogen peroxide should be used. If there is a discharge, or bad odor is detected, the dog may be suffering from infection or mite infestation. In such a case, the ear must also be treated with proper medication.

Teeth should be cleaned with a doggy or baby brush. A dry brush is excellent for this purpose, or a bit of gauze wrapped around the finger. Now is the time to check the dog's teeth for cavities or retained teeth. Discovering double or retained baby teeth in a Chinese Crested puppy older than four months warrants a veterinary visit to surgically remove them; otherwise, they can cause serious dental problems and even a wry mouth, when one side of the jaw grows longer than the other side.

Shaving and Trimming

Before bathing, the Hairless Crested ought to be shaved if it has any body hair. The Powderpuff needs to be combed to remove mats. To protect ears from water getting inside and potential infection, they should be plugged with earplugs or cotton balls.

All grooming should start with nail clipping and ear cleaning.

The Tub

Finally the question: where to bathe the dog? The kitchen sink will accommodate a young Crested puppy, but once the dog grows up, a sink will be too small to do a good job. Bathtubs would be great if not for the fact that, because of their low level, bending over can be difficult for the owner.

Laundry tubs, which can be bought in any hardware store, are excellent alternatives to expensive pet tubs and considerably less costly. They are made of plastic and supplied with legs that stand inside a regular bathtub at a level comfortable for the owner. All have a drain hole and sometimes extra water ports or eyebolts to which a restraint or harness can be attached.

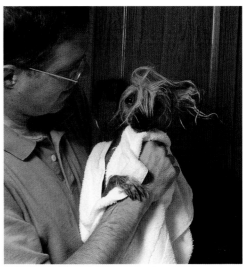

The kitchen sink can be used to bathe a small Crested.

Bathing and Cleaning

Bathing the Hairless Crested

The skin of your Hairless Crested should be gently scrubbed with a buff puff or a loofah sponge. The water should be just warm enough for him to feel comfortable, as water that is too hot can cause the dog great discomfort. It is important to avoid getting soapsuds in your Crested's eyes, as it may cause irritation and eye ulcers.

Because the toes of the Chinese Crested Hairless dog contain sebaceous and sweat glands, the spaces between them must be deeply massaged, preferably with sulfur soap, to prevent cysts or warts.

Although there are many different shampoos on the market, the best ones for the Hairless Crested are certified hypoallergenic and made with natural botanical ingredients. Shampoo containing colloidal oatmeal is excellent for a dog suffering from skin irritations or chaffing. Selsun Blue shampoo is a good remedy for seborrhea and oily skin.

Treating Infected Skin

Infected skin will improve dramatically with the application of fresh carrot juice. A towel is dipped in carrot juice and applied to the skin for about ten minutes each time, then rinsed with warm water.

Dry skin loves papaya and strawberry masks. Mashed fruit is mixed with couple of teaspoons (9 g) of yogurt, then put on the skin and covered with plastic wrap. After 15 minutes, the

---

WARNING
Chinese Crested puppies can get pneumonia if cold or wet. Do not bathe puppies less than eight weeks old!

Papaya and strawberry masks can enhance the beauty of your Crested's skin.

covering is removed and the dog is encouraged to eat some of the mush, as it is tasty and healthful. The remaining residue is washed off with warm water. Other fruit can be used, too. However, citrus should be applied only to oily skin or in case of acne. Masks are usually done once a week.

Bathing the Powderpuff Crested

The Powderpuff's coat has to be carefully hand washed to prevent hair breakage. It should be washed and rinsed twice. A good conditioner is applied next, to prevent matting. A capful of fabric softener per gallon (3.8 L) of warm water is used sometimes as a final rinse to prevent static. The coat is first dried with a towel, then with a dryer set to medium–low heat, blowing the hair toward the head and downward.

Oily skin should be cleansed with cotton wipes dipped in witch hazel lotion or Oxy pads.

Show Dogs

All Chinese Cresteds who participate in confirmation shows must be groomed and conditioned daily. There is simply no escape from this duty. Many great dogs have failed to achieve championship status only because their owners either did not know how to groom them properly or did not understand the concept of a ring presentation.

Puppies

Very young puppies should not be bathed because of the danger of pneumonia. If the situation requires washing a puppy younger than six weeks, only a waterless shampoo, soap- and detergent-free, should be used. Miracle Coat Waterless Shampoo and Tearless Shampoo are both safe for Crested puppies and can be easily obtained online or from mail-order catalogs. The shampoo is first sprayed on the coat or skin, and then left to set. Once the dirt is dissolved, it is brushed out from the coat or, in the case of a Hairless puppy, wiped from the skin with a clean towel.

Grooming the Powderpuff

The biggest challenge in grooming a long, silky coat are the mats, which often form around the legs, ears, and side of the face. For this reason alone, the Chinese Crested Powderpuff, particularly if competing in a show ring, must be brushed and conditioned regularly.

Although the Powderpuff is much less demanding than his hairless brother, keeping the dog's coat in good condition involves work.

Between shows, the coat has to be oiled to prevent matting and breakage. The oil solution used by most handlers is made from a teaspoon (5 mL) of coat oil (coat oil made specifically for dogs can be bought online from pet supply web sites) mixed with ½ gallon (2 L) of warm water, with which the entire coat is well saturated and then dried slowly with a blow dryer. This routine is done daily. The day before the show, the dog's face, beard, and ears (unless the fringes are desired) have to be shaved with a trimmer using a very fine surgical blade. The whole face, including the whiskers, is shaved very closely from ear to ear, leaving a little tuft of hair in the shape of a letter V between the eyes. Next, the skin below the eyes and around the lips is stretched and shaved again to make sure that all hair is removed. Then a shaving pattern is marked on the neck to be followed later with a clipper. The V's sharp point begins just below the Adam's apple at the nape of the neck.

If desired, the ears are shaved with the same surgical blade, taking care not to cut them accidentally. Hair is removed from the outside and the inside of the ears. Then the coat is combed gently to remove any mats (a dining fork does a great job of removing individual mats!) and is ready for a bath. All trace of conditioning oil must be removed, which means the coat needs to be washed and rinsed at least twice. Finally, a conditioner is applied and the hair is rinsed again. A capful of fabric softener per gallon (3.8 L) of warm water as a final rinse will prevent static. The coat is first dried with a towel, then with a dryer set to medium-low heat, blowing the hair toward the head and downward.

HOW –TO: GROOM THE

Your Chinese Crested Hairless, with his long furnishings, is usually a very hairy dog requiring elaborate grooming to give the impression of being truly naked. Indeed, the glamorous Chinese Crested Hairless dogs seen in magazines and books are shaved-down hairy dogs whose owners spend hours to create the correct look. The crest does not end at the neckline but continues all the way to the tail and down the legs, joining with the socks. Sometimes even the chest is covered with hair!

These step-by-step instructions are for pet owners and show exhibitors alike.

First, all unwanted hair from the Hairless Crested dog's body needs to be removed. This is done by using a trimmer as close to the skin as possible. Next, the dog has to be bathed. A hair dryer or a towel can be used to dry the dog. Once this part is accomplished, the dog will have to be placed on a sturdy, nonskid surface for further grooming.

For shaving the face, a small trimmer, such as a Wahl Peanut, is used with a very fine or surgical blade, either #40 or #50. These blades are very sharp; therefore, it is important to keep the dog still to prevent injury, particularly to the eyes. Because many Chinese Cresteds intensely dislike being shaved, you must be prepared for him to fight, particularly when it comes to doing the face.

The Chinese Crested Hairless dog has an elongated hare foot.

There are two ways to shave the face: the first style requires shaving the face all the way to the ears, and the second style involves shaving the face only to the eye corners, leaving the sideburns intact.

Shaving the ears is optional. If your dog has very strong, fully erect ears, removal of hair fringes can be left to personal preference. However, if he has weak or floppy ears, he will have to have all the hair removed to train the ears to stand up and allow them to be taped. A perfectly shaped crest should start at the junction of the neck with the trunk. Using a heavy-duty clipper such as a Futura or Oster A1, the excess hair on the dog's body is shaved off, starting from the neckline and

The face can be shaved all the way to the ears.

The face is shaved, leaving the sideburns intact.

going all the way to the tail and down the abdominal area. Next, the hair is removed from the shoulders, upper arms, elbows, and chest, then from the buttocks, stifles, and thighs. Hair on the pasterns and hocks are called socks and left intact. The length of the socks on the pasterns should be on the same level with the socks on the hocks. Finally, the socks are shaped neatly with scissors, forming an inverted V to emphasize the characteristic elongated hare foot of the Hairless Crested.

Any hair growing between the toes on the footpad should be removed with scissors or a trimmer.

If the dog has any hair growing on the chest or abdomen, it will need to be removed, too.

Tail trimming is next. Starting from the base, at least 2 inches (5 cm) or one-fifth of the plume should be taken off in accordance with the requirement of the Standard.

Now that the dog has been correctly shaved, the next task is to remove the remaining hair stubs so that the skin will feel perfectly smooth and "truly hairless." Depilatories or similar chemical products should never be used for this purpose, as they can cause severe burns and allergic reactions. A Braun shaver should be used instead. It is not only safer, but while shaving, it eliminates blackheads and retained hair roots, which if not removed regularly often become infected. During the shaving process, the skin should be stretched and the shaver held against it at a 90-degree angle. The head of the shaver should be moved slowly back and forth, pressing against the skin until it feels velvety smooth to the touch. Once grooming is finished, a hot oil treatment can be applied to the furnishings to add volume. Later, the dog

The shaving pattern for the hairy Hairless dog.

will have to be bathed again, but this time with beauty shampoo, followed by conditioner. If the furnishings, particularly the socks, look too yellow or are stained, #1 All Systems Super Whitening Gel will remove discoloration. This gel will also wash out any facial stains caused by excessive tearing. Finally, Emu oil or another good moisturizer is applied to the skin to give it a shiny look and protect it from dryness.

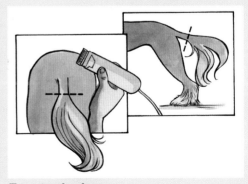

Trimming the plume.

TRAINING THE CHINESE CRESTED

Training the Chinese Crested dog can be a challenge because of her stubbornness. But if you appeal to your dog's intelligence using the right training method, even the most obnoxious Crested can become a model dog.

Basic Obedience Training

Dogs are social animals, and without proper training, they will act like wild beasts, soiling the house and damaging the furniture, barking wildly, biting, or fighting other dogs. Still, what their owners tend to get upset about and consider bad behavior are perfectly normal canine actions that happen to occur at the wrong time or in the wrong setting. The solution to preventing behavior problems lies in learning how to teach your dog to redirect her instinctual tendencies to activities you consider acceptable. Because Chinese Cresteds have a propensity toward self-indulgence, they benefit from regular obedience training. The training establishes the social hierarchy where you are

Training sessions should be short and fun for your dog.

the master, instead of your dog. In addition, obeying such simple commands as *sit, heel,* or *stay* can save a dog's life. For example, if your dog gets lost in the middle of a street, she can be safely heeled across and then given a *sit* command to wait to be retrieved.

The single most important aspect of training is rewarding the dog for good behavior. At the same time, the dog should never be punished if she forgets. A reprimand is all that is needed. Chinese Cresteds are very sensitive to their owners' moods and know by the tone of their voices when they displease them. Hitting with a newspaper, or pulling and twisting the ear, is a terrible thing to do to a dog and will only make her more aggressive, making existing problems worse and creating additional ones.

Training requires patience, consistency, a collar, a leash, and an understanding of dog

A correct reprimand is a quick "No."
Physical punishment is never allowed!

behavior. It usually begins by teaching the dog to walk on a lead. Basic commands can be taught in any language and always include *heel, halt, sit, stay, down, come,* and a sharp *no*. Additionally, the dog should learn such terms as *quiet, off, wait,* and *stop it*. The sessions should be short and interesting, so that they can become the dog's favorite activity.

One of the finest training methods uses a clicker to praise a dog for good behavior. Karen Pryor, a behavioral biologist, has developed this method. Instead of a voice, the clicker is used to reinforce good behavior and to get the dog's attention. Each time your dog does something correctly, you should click the clicker and offer her a treat.

Another method also uses a clicker, although not to send a praise signal, but as a communication tool. You need to decide in advance on the number of clicks you will assign to each behavior. For example, if you assign two clicks to *sit*, you should first show the dog what you want her to do and then click twice when the dog successfully passes the test. The practice should take place every day at the same time and in the same spot, away from any noise or interference. A treat is given immediately after the clicks. Eventually, the verbal command is eliminated and instead the dog is "told" what to do by merely pressing the appropriate number of clicks. When one behavior is accomplished, you and your dog can move on to the next one. Because a dog's memory is short, it is better to use this method with a maximum of five to six basic commands. *No* is always verbal. Because of the limited range of "clicked" commands, this method of training is best for show dogs to teach them how to act in the ring.

Well-behaved Chinese Crested dogs may be eligible for an award from the American Kennel Club. The Canine Good Citizen (CGC) program, which started in 1989, is designed to award well-behaved dogs. To receive the Canine Good Citizen award, you and your dog must pass the CGC test. The assessment involves judging the dog's attitudes and responses to different situations, and her grooming and appearance.

Many Chinese Cresteds excel in agility trials.

*To successfully communicate with your dog,
you need to come down to her level.*

The Problem Chinese Crested

Most behavioral problems with Chinese Cresteds are related to their excessive submissiveness or stubbornness. Submissive urination is common among Chinese Cresteds, and even though it may be repulsive to the owners, it is a perfectly natural behavior among dogs. Dogs have several behaviors that nature intended to minimize hostility between them. A challenged submissive dog must display certain behavior to demonstrate its lower status and prevent being attacked. Submissive urination is the commonly offered gesture to the alpha dog and is designed to generate a friendly response. Thus, scolding a dog for submissive urinating will make it even more afraid.

Another mistake the owner can make is to try to establish eye contact with such a dog. For a submissive Chinese Crested, this can be unendurable, since it shows dominance on the part of the owner. Even patting on the head can invoke a panic attack in a submissive dog and, of course, urination. To treat the problem, you should avoid making any threatening gestures to your dog.

Some Chinese Crested owners reported success with their problem pets by using touch therapy. The Tellington TTouch, a specialized form of touch therapy, was developed by animal expert Linda Tellington-Jones. TTouch uses circular movements of the fingers and hands over the dog's entire body—including the face, lips, and gums. Because many Cresteds can be very

sensitive to touch, it is best for you to start at her chin and then move downward toward her chest and legs. Once your dog is comfortable with this, the rest of her body can be massaged, including the head, face, and gums.

Many owners complain that their Chinese Cresteds are "stubborn" or that they "refuse to listen" when given a command. However, before blaming the dog, you must first honestly determine whether you have created the problem by sending your dog mixed signals. When a verbal command signifies one thing, but a gesture another, the dog will be too confused to understand what is expected and will disobey the command.

A show prospect Chinese Crested should learn the art of "free stacking."

Another problem occasionally encountered in Chinese Crested dogs is aggressiveness, particularly toward strangers. There are many causes of aggression in dogs, from abusive treatment by their owners, bad social relationships, and fright, to dominance, jealousy, and territoriality. Very rarely is the cause genetic. If aggressiveness is caused by an illness, it usually resolves itself once the dog gets better. All cases of aggression must be decided on an individual basis, as the treatment depends on the cause. However, you should leave the problem to a professional behaviorist, and not attempt to solve it yourself.

A respected trainer once said, "Where the head goes, the body will follow." It is true!

Training for the Show

To become an AKC champion, the dog must
• earn a minimum of 15 points;
• twice earn 3 or more points (a "major") in a show, each under two different judges;
• earn at least 1 point under a third judge.

Training a puppy for the show ring should begin very early. Charlotte Ventura, a handler and trainer of various breeds of dogs, including Chinese Cresteds, advocates starting the training practice at eight weeks of age. The following program describes her method, which has been used with great success on many top-winning dogs.

The puppy should first be trained in the home, but as soon as she has had all required vaccinations, she must be taken around and introduced to as many strangers as possible, as well as to a variety of different places. Early socialization is the foundation for a good show dog, especially the Chinese Crested.

As soon as the show-prospect puppy arrives home, the owner, pretending to be the judge, should inspect her fully by checking the dog's entire body, just as is done at shows. The puppy's teeth must be scrutinized, too. This is done by lifting her upper lip and exposing her top teeth to check for a proper bite. In the case of a male dog, both testicles should be firmly in the scrotum. (Judges will check that to be sure both are there.) A dog will encounter these things in the show ring. Many judges equate lack of socialization with poor temperament and will not reward even the most beautiful dog if she displays shyness in the show ring.

Once the puppy is introduced to the world, it is time to start basic training for the show ring. Training the puppy on an elevated surface, such as a countertop or table, will provide good footing (a bath towel works well) and expose the dog to the show routine, since Chinese Cresteds are always examined by the judge on a grooming table.

You must be careful, however, because one bad experience on the table can cause a dog to hate the show ring, fearing a repeat of that experience. Purchasing an inexpensive grooming table is good not only for training, but for future grooming as well. Alternating surfaces is ideal. The various kennel clubs holding the shows will often have grooming tables with varying surfaces.

Next comes selecting a favorite small treat or toy (fuzzy/squeaky toys work well) that the puppy would enjoy using during training time. The show ring should be the ONLY place the

TIP

Show Ring Patterns

The usual patterns used in all show rings are as follows:
- A straight line
- A triangle
- A circle

dog will be rewarded with that particular treat or toy, outside the training sessions. This makes it all the more special to the puppy. Once the puppy is comfortable on the elevated surface, you should reward her with a treat. At this point you should begin "stacking" your puppy on the table. *Stacking* is a term used by show people and means placing your dog's legs in a show position. Ideally, the front legs will be placed directly under the body, with the feet pointing straight ahead and the head held up. The back legs are then placed so that the hock is perpendicular to the ground or table and the toes are forward. In this position, when viewed from the side, your dog should have a perfect profile. Experienced handlers can stack a dog with a variety of faults, making her look perfect when viewed on the table.

Each training session should not last longer than ten minutes, regardless of whether it concerns working with a young puppy on stacking or any other skill. The puppy must enjoy every practice and consider it fun, as too much of anything can lead to boredom. Once the dog is standing well in a stacked position, she should be praised effusively and offered her favorite treat. Training for ten minutes at a time, a few

the dog to strike that winning pose. This is how it all begins.

Next, it is time to teach the puppy to walk on a show lead. It is important to remember that all dogs are unique and that one may do better on one type of lead, whereas another does better on something very different. A ¼-inch (5-mm) Rescoe lead is commonly used on toy dogs. Chinese Cresteds often respond best to a lightweight type of lead. Some dogs have sensitive throats and, in such case, the owner may want to try something called a "kindness" lead. The "kindness" lead has a small pad that just covers the dog's throat.

In the very beginning, putting the leash on in the house and letting the puppy run around (supervised) to get used to the feeling of the lead around the neck is all that is required. You should be prepared for a "puppy tantrum" when you take the other end of the lead in your hand. The puppy may scream, roll, gag, try to grab the lead, or just plain lie down and refuse to go. However, keeping a happy voice and a pocket full of treats will soon calm the dog down. Soon the dog will be walking right by your side . . . which is, of course, always the LEFT side.

Once walking has been mastered, the lead should be gathered in the left hand, leaving just enough slack to feel comfortable. The right hand should hold that trusty treat. Now the dog should be guided with the treat, taking her in the direction she is supposed to go. At first, your back might become sore from bending over to puppy level, but once the dog realizes that treats are in hand, you can begin walking upright, having the dog focused on your right hand.

times a day, makes the time fun and productive for both you and your puppy.

The next very important step is to teach the puppy the art of "free stacking." If stacking is a correct placement of the feet, *free stacking* means that the dog will do it all by itself. This behavior should be taught early. The dog is shown her favorite treat to help her focus on your face. She will need to stand in front of you and look at you as if you are all that matters to her. When the dog stands, looking up at you, she should be praised lavishly and rewarded with a treat. This may all seem a little silly at first, but anyone who has ever watched Best in Show at Westminster on television would recognize the moment when it is up to

Finding a place to practice walking with the dog in these patterns is the next task.

Your puppy's attitude is measured by her tail when moving in the show ring. Judges want to see a happy dog with good tail carriage. Once again, few will reward the dog that keeps its tail between its legs on the move. Using a happy voice when moving the dog will usually encourage your dog to pick up her tail.

Now free stacking should be incorporated with the above show patterns. At the completion of the pattern, you should turn to your dog, treat in hand, and let her stand and look at you for a few seconds. This done, the practice should be finished off with praise and a treat.

Eventually in the show ring you will be asked to move your dog, and when you come back to the judge, you will have only those few precious seconds to convince him or her that your dog is the best. While the dog is gazing into your eyes eagerly awaiting that treat, the judge will walk around the dog and judge her while she is on the ground. This method of free stacking will also be used while the dog is lined up with the other dogs in her class and the judge is looking at them as a group. The judge may also come down the line of dogs and look at their facial expressions. You must be ready for the judge by having your dog already posed, eyes fixated on the special treat.

It is important to do all this training outside of the ring. When your puppy has been raised with these simple methods of "play training," she will be ready to face any situation when she enters the ring.

To encourage a positive attitude, the puppy should be passed off EARLY to strangers. Ask them to hold the dog while you pretend to walk away for a minute or two. Do not make any fuss when returning, even if the puppy begs for it. In addition, when you are practicing on a table, other people should be invited to examine the pup as a judge would. Judges come in all shapes, sizes, and nationalities. Some might wear hats or glasses. Others are very tall and threatening. The point is to expose your dog to various people before she goes into the show ring. To make sure that each experience is pleasant, the strangers handling the dog should be furnished with that special treat to reward her.

It is also important to expose the puppy to other dogs since they will be in front of or behind her in the show ring at one time or another. Other exhibitors may not be as courteous as they ought to be, so getting the dog used to having another dog following closely behind is very important.

Lastly, any show prospect must be socialized with other breeds. Chinese Cresteds know their own breed but may be uncomfortable with other breeds, large and small. After all, the day may come when your puppy will be the only Chinese Crested in the Best in Show lineup at the end of the day!

THE CHINESE CRESTED'S HEALTH

The Chinese Crested breed is still considered rare in many places, and not every veterinarian has enough knowledge or experience, particularly regarding the Hairless variety, to give accurate advice about care or behavioral problems. Powderpuffs can be mistaken for the Havanese or Maltese, and a natural hairlessness in the naked variety can be diagnosed as a medical condition, such as alopecia. In addition, very hairy Hairless dogs are occasionally misidentified as Powderpuffs.

It must be stressed that the majority of Chinese Crested dogs are very healthy animals with cheerful dispositions. However, dogs, just like people, suffer from illnesses and various defects, and you should not expect something that you do not expect of yourself. Just because a dog is purebred, or comes from

Finding a competent veterinarian familiar with Chinese Cresteds is a very important task, as the life of the dog may depend on his knowledge of the breed.

a reputable kennel and has a guarantee clause in the contract, does not mean that she will always remain healthy or free of defects. Such assumptions are unfair to the breeder and unfair to the dog. Very few genetic tests are available to the breeders of Chinese Cresteds, but even if they had all kinds of tests at their disposal, it would be impossible to find a dog entirely free of problems. There has never been a perfect dog and never will be. Let us just hope that this realization may help all Crested owners to value their dogs more, not less.

Preventive Health Care

Vaccines

According to recent studies, it is not necessary to repeat DHPP vaccinations annually, but at three-year intervals. DHPP stands for "distemper, hepatitis, parainfluenza, and parvovirus." Vaccines for dogs are divided into two classes. "Core" vaccines are those that should be given to every Chinese Crested. "Noncore" vaccines are recommended only for dogs in certain circumstances. The decision depends on the lifestyle of the dog and her potential exposure to disease. The AVMA Council on Biologic and Therapeutic Agents' 2003 Report on Cat and Dog Vaccines has recommended that core vaccines for dogs include only those for distemper, canine adenovirus-2 (hepatitis and respiratory disease), and canine parvovirus-2.

Vaccines considered noncore are those for leptospirosis, coronavirus, canine parainfluenza

You need to weigh the benefits and risks of noncore vaccines.

TIP

A Life Well-Lived

Overall, the Chinese Crested is a hardy and long-lived dog, often reaching the ripe age of 16 or more, providing she receives adequate care, diet, and attention from her owner.

---

and Bordetella bronchiseptica (both are causes of "kennel cough"), and Borrelia burgdorferi (causing Lyme disease).

A series of vaccinations beginning at 8 weeks and given 3 to 4 weeks apart, up to 16 weeks of age, is all that a young puppy requires. Another vaccination given after 6 months of age (usually at 1 year, 4 months) is believed to provide long-term immunity. Many researchers at veterinary schools also suggest using single-component vaccines instead of a combination against more than one disease. (Cole, R. Rethinking canine vaccinations. *Veterinary Forum*, Jan. 1998, 52–57.)

The most dangerous of the contagious viral diseases are parvovirus and distemper, which are the number one killers of puppies and young dogs worldwide. The early signs of parvovirus are not specific. Any signs of lethargy and loss of appetite progressing within two days to vomiting and bloody or green diarrhea with a high fever calls for immediate action and contacting the veterinarian. Canine distemper, just like parvovirus, is usually transmitted through contact

Vaccination Schedule

Age	Vaccine Recommended
8 weeks	Parvo (MLV) and Distemper (MLV)
11–12 weeks	DHPP
15–16 weeks	DHPP, Rabies (Killed)
1 year and 4 months	Rabies (Killed), DHPP

Talk to your veterinarian about vaccinating your puppy.

with saliva, fecal material, or urine. Symptoms are similar to those of a cold or influenza.

Bordetella, a noncore vaccine, is mainly recommended only for those Cresteds who are boarded or attending dog shows, or whenever exposed to many unknown dogs. Immunity requires 72 hours, is of short duration, and does not protect from every cause of kennel cough.

Coronavirus is a rare, self-limiting disease affecting puppies less than eight weeks old. Cornell University and Texas A&M University have diagnosed only one case in the last seven years.

Leptospirosis is a kidney infection contracted from water contaminated by wild animals. The vaccine is a common cause of adverse reactions in Chinese Cresteds and is immunosuppressive to puppies younger than 16 weeks old. Protection is short lived, and the risk of side effects outweighs benefits.

Vaccinations may fail if they are improperly administered, past the validity date, or damaged. In addition, they may fail if a dog suffers from an immunological disorder, is malnourished, or has been already exposed to the illness. Also, reactions to vaccines sometimes happen after an injection. Signs of anaphylactic shock include nausea, diarrhea, skin rush or hives, swelling of the lips and eyelids, staggering gait, and glossy eyes.

Internal and External Parasites

Most Crested puppies have intestinal worms, as the dam often will infect them with her dormant worm larvae during pregnancy. Puppies should be dewormed at five weeks and again at seven and nine weeks, as some immunity to intestinal parasites comes only after five to seven months of age.

Another danger to dogs is heartworm infection. Even the youngest of puppies can be infected with a heartworm larva transmitted by a mosquito bite. The adult heartworm often reaches a size of 6 to 14 inches (15–35 cm).

Worm Symptoms

Worm	Symptoms
Roundworms	Pot belly, vomiting, diarrhea or loose stool, weight loss
Hookworms	anemia, diarrhea, bloody stools (especially in puppies)
Tapeworms	rarely seen, possible diarrhea/vomiting
Whipworms	loss of weight, fetid diarrhea
Threadworms	profuse watery diarrhea, breathing difficulties (esp. puppies)

A dog may have several hundred of these worms clogging its heart before they finally kill the dog. Signs of heartworm disease are frequent coughing, sluggishness, tiring, and hard breathing.

The ordinary flea is the leading cause of skin problems in the Chinese Crested. Most dogs that are bitten by fleas will have only irritation or itching, but some may develop a severe allergic skin condition called flea allergy dermatitis. Fleas also carry the tapeworm larvae in their saliva, which they introduce into the bloodstream of the host dog.

Ticks are the cause of Lyme disease, ehrlichiosis, and Rocky Mountain spotted fever. Immediate signs of Lyme disease include fever and joint pain, progressing often to heart and kidney disease. Clinical signs of ehrlichiosis, which is transmitted by a brown tick, may include bleeding disorders, an enlarged spleen, difficulty breathing, weight loss, and perhaps neurological signs. Rocky Mountain's symptoms, in addition to fever, swelling of the limbs, and pneumonia, may also include neurological signs.

Mites are a common cause of ear and skin problems in the Chinese Crested. These parasites can usually be found inside and around the dog's ears or, if the Demodex type, usually on the trunk and face. The most common sign of ear mite infection is a shaking of the head and ears. Black debris accumulates in the ears of infected pets, causing them intense discomfort.

Common chiggers, also known as "jiggers," are usually encountered in late spring and summer. Chiggers insert their mouthparts into a skin pore or hair follicle and inject a salivary secretion containing powerful digestive enzymes. Their "bites" produce small, reddish welts on the skin accompanied by intense itching.

Toxins

A Chinese Crested is a very curious little dog and will try to eat anything that looks or smells interesting. Your dog may climb onto your dining table or even sneak into food cabinets. When outside, the Crested will not hesitate to eat things that she finds palatable. Unfortunately, some toxic things can be very tasty. Here is a general list of poisons that can affect the Chinese Crested:

Sugarless candies
Salmon poisoning
Alcohol
Onions and garlic

Grapes and raisins
Ibuprofen
Chemical toxins
Napthalene or mothballs
Chocolate
Antifreeze (ethylene glycol)
Organophosphate in fertilizers and weed killers
House and garden plants
Toad poisoning
Lead poisoning
Sugarless candies containing xylitol can be toxic to pets. Xylitol can cause liver damage and death in susceptible dogs.

Salmon poisoning is a problem mainly in the Pacific Northwest and California. It is caused by an infection from a tiny organism called *Neorickettsia helminthoeca* that is found in contaminated fish. A sudden onset of symptoms occurs five to seven days after ingestion. Initial symptoms include lethargy and loss of appetite. The dog's temperature goes up to 104–107°F (40–42°C) in the first two days and then slowly returns to normal. Persistent vomiting happens by the fourth or fifth day, followed by bloody diarrhea. The diarrhea is often bright yellow or green. There are enlarged lymph nodes as well. In the acute stages, gastrointestinal symptoms are quite similar to canine parvovirus, and nasal and ocular symptoms can resemble canine distemper. If left untreated, salmon poisoning has a mortality rate of up to 90 percent. Dogs that survive are immune to the toxin for life. The disease can be prevented by cooking all fish before feeding the Crested and removing snails from the garden or lawn.

Onion toxicity is common in dogs. The Crested can develop hemolytic anemia if it eats enough onions. It does not matter whether the onions are cooked or not. Large amounts of

Some household plants can be harmful to your dog. Check with your local poison control center for a complete list.

garlic can produce similar effects, but a small amount does not seem to be a problem.

Grapes and raisins are cherished by some Cresteds, so poisonings can happen easily. The gastrointestinal signs include vomiting and diarrhea and then signs of kidney failure, with an onset of severe kidney signs starting about 24 hours after ingestion. Because of the severity of the symptoms and the potential for death, aggressive medical treatment is advocated for any dog suspected of eating large amounts of grapes or raisins.

Poisonous mushrooms can cause severe liver disease and neurological disorders.

———— **T I P** ————

Poisoning

If you suspect that your Crested has been poisoned, you should call the ASPCA poison control hotline immediately at (888) 4ANI-HELP or (888) 426-4435.

Antifreeze poisoning from ethylene glycol happens often, usually because of human neglect. The antifreeze compounds contain toxic ethylene glycol, which seems to be very palatable to many Cresteds. Even one teaspoonful of antifreeze (5 mL) can kill a 7-pound (3-kg) Crested within 30 minutes of ingestion. Depression, signs of intoxication similar to alcohol ingestion, vomiting, depression, tremor, coma, and even death may occur among the initial signs of poisoning. For a dog to survive, treatment must be initiated within five hours of ingestion. For the sake of one's Crested pet, it may be a good idea to switch to antifreeze brands that do not contain ethylene glycol and are considered safer for pets.

Ibuprofen is toxic for the Chinese Crested. One 200-mg tablet can cause stomach ulcers in a small dog of 5–7 pounds (2.2–3 kg), and six tablets, kidney failure.

Hazardous and Toxic Plants

Hazardous and toxic plants include tomato leaves and stems; potato leaves and stems; green lily bulbs, onions, onion powder, rhubarb leaves, hops, macadamia nuts, mistletoe berries (just two or three berries could be fatal to a small dog), poinsettia (an irritant), azalea, castor bean, datura, oleander, sago palm, yews (very dangerous), philodendron, azalea, rhododendron, sansevieria, snake plant, schefflera, umbrella tree, Jerusalem cherry, water hemlock, dogbane, horse nettle, buffalo bur, rattle box, purple sesbane, coffee bean, corn cockle, milkweeds, poison hemlock, yellow jessamine, evening trumpet, Carolina jessamine, ivy bush, lambskill, caladium, angel wings, spider plant, St. Bernard's lily, airplane plant, cyclamen, snowbread, shooting star, dumbcane, foxglove, dragon tree, English holly, European holly, kalanchoe, cathedral bells, daffodils, and hyacinths. Many of these plants are poisonous only when consumed; others have vicious barbs that sting or snare your helpless pet. This list is not complete. For more information, check with your local poison control center.

Poisons

Organophosphate is an ingredient of many insect killers, ant poisons, and flea powders, and some fertilizer and lawn remedies. Organophosphate poisoning has certain signs, such as excessive salivation, diarrhea, slow heart rate, and pinpoint pupils, that distinguish it from other conditions.

Chocolate contains a xanthine compound, theobromine, which is toxic in sufficient quantities. Examples of other xanthine compounds are caffeine and theophylline. The toxicity from all these compounds is similar. Using a dose of 100 mg/kg as the toxic dose, the toxic dosages per pound of body weight for Cresteds are as follows:

1 ounce (30 g) per pound (454 g) of body weight for milk chocolate

1 ounce (30 g) per 3 pounds (1.5 kg) of body weight for semisweet chocolate

1 ounce (30 g) per 9 pounds (4 kg) of body weight for baker's chocolate

*Healthy snacks for your Chinese Crested
include dog bones, not chocolate.*

The toxic signs include extreme excitability or irritability, increased heart rate, restlessness, increased urination, vomiting, and tremors. Severe intoxication can lead to death. Inducing vomiting and administering activated charcoal can help if the ingestion has occurred within two hours. Severe cases will need hospitalization and supportive therapy. Diarrhea may be an additional common problem. This often occurs 12 to 24 hours after eating the chocolate.

Arsenic can be found in some rodenticides, weed killers, wood preservatives, insecticides, baits, and even some tick dips.

Lead poisoning is extremely common in the environment. Linoleum, caulk, lead-based paints, lead pencils, bullets, golf balls, solder, batteries, lead putty, fishing weights, and other items around the home or in the garage that a Crested may encounter can contain lead.

Snakes, Toads, Spiders, and Lizards

Several species of giant toads are a serious threat to the Chinese Crested. When toads are threatened, glands in their skin secrete a white, milky mixture of poisons. Symptoms of toad poisoning in dogs can include heavy drooling, foaming at the mouth, head shaking, vomiting, bloody diarrhea, bright red or very pale gums, paralysis, loss of coordination, fever, irregular or very fast heartbeat, difficult breathing, tightly clamped jaws, seizures, and even death.

The Gila monster is the largest lizard in the United States and is found in the desert regions of Arizona, western New Mexico, southeastern California, the southern tip of Nevada, the extreme southwest region of Utah, and northwestern Mex-

ico. The usual place of bite is the upper lip. If the Gila monster bites a Crested, the dog may require medical supportive treatment and antibiotic therapy. There is no antivenin available. The best way to avoid a bite from a poisonous lizard is to prevent the dog from roaming.

Snake poisoning is a real emergency! Even a small snake may give a fatal bite. The commonly encountered venomous snakes in North America are viperine and include the puff adder, the russel viper, and the European adder, and the pit vipers such as the rattlesnake, cottonmouth moccasin or water moccasin, and copperhead. Only immediate medical help can save a dog's life.

Spider bites may cause pain, swelling, and infection. The spiders to be most concerned about are the widows, such as the black widow, characterized by the red hourglass on her abdomen, the western black widow, the brown widow common to the South, and the red widow common to Florida. Widow spiders inject extemely toxic venom. The clinical signs of a bite are painful cramping of the muscles. Recovery may be prolonged, with some weakness and even a slight paralysis persisting for several days. Brown spiders can be recognized by a violin-shaped marking on the body, but not always. Within four to eight hours, a bull's-eye marking appears around the bite, with the center appearing white or pale. This may degenerate into an open sore or ulcer. The tissue damage may take weeks to heal.

Other Common Dangers

Foxtails are wild grasses resembling the tails of foxes and are usually found only in states west of the Mississippi River and in Southern California. The seeds of the dried grasses often lodge in the feet or in the furnishings, between the dog's toes, inside the ears, or even the eyes. Because the seeds are barbed like fishhooks, they can be very difficult to remove. Once embedded, foxtail seeds cause severe infections and abscesses. If swallowed, foxtail seeds will cause severe inflammation and swelling of the throat, making it quite painful and difficult for the dog to eat or drink. Deeply embedded foxtails have to be surgically removed by a skilled veterinarian.

Swallowing foreign objects seems to be another favorite pastime of some Cresteds, particularly puppies. Only a skilled veterinarian can remove most large sharp objects in the throat. Attempting to remove the object oneself can make the situation worse.

Taking Your Dog's Temperature

Although the skin of your Hairless Crested may feel very warm to the touch, her body temperature is the same as any other dog. The normal temperature for the Crested, Hairless and Powderpuff varieties alike, ranges from 99.5 to 102.5°F (37.5 to 39°C). A variety of digital thermometers to measure body temperature are available. The tip of the thermometer should be lubricated with petroleum jelly and slowly inserted into the rectum.

Emergency Medical Kit

Every Chinese Crested owner should have emergency medical supplies on hand. The basic kit should consist of the following:
(1) Thermometer
(1) Sterile lubricant
(6) 2-by-2-inch (5-by-5-cm) gauze bandages
(6) 3-by-3-inch (8-by-8-cm) gauze bandages
(1) 2-inch-by-12-foot (5-cm-by-3.6-m) conforming gauze roll bandage
(1) 3-inch-by-12-foot (8-cm-by-3.6-m) conforming gauze roll bandage
(1) Burn-relief gel pack
(6) Antiseptic cleansing wipes
(1) 4 oz. (120 mL) hydrogen peroxide
(1) 1-inch-by-18-foot (2.5-cm-by-4.5-m) first aid tape
(3) Antibiotic ointment packs
(1) Iodine
(1) Forceps
(1) Scissors
(1) Bag of cotton balls
(1) Condensed or powdered milk
(1) Box of Oxy pads
(1) Sunscreen lotion for your hairless Crested
(1) Eyedrops such as Visine or eye lubricant
(1) Benadryl
(1) Packet of cotton swabs
(1) Paper towels
(1) Emergency telephone numbers for poison control and your veterinarian
(1) Sulfur ointment
(1) Sulfur soap

(1) Flowers of sulfur if living in or visiting an area where chiggers are a problem
(2) Long-sleeve shirt and pants

Digestive System

There are many causes of the Crested's digestive disorders—from sudden changes in diet and overeating to ingestion of garbage, infection (bacterial or viral), inflammatory bowel disease, and cancer. Bacterial diseases include *Campylobacter jejuni*, varieties of salmonella, and *Escherichia coli*, an organism that may be present without causing problems until the Crested dog becomes stressed. Since *C. jejuni* and salmonella can infect humans, washing hands carefully after handling a sick pet is strongly advised. Viral causes of diarrhea include distemper, corona, and parvovirus. Parasitic causes of diarrhea include giardia, coccidia, hookworms, and whipworms. Giardia and coccidia are protozoa, tiny one-celled animals. They are the most common cause of bloody diarrhea in puppies.

Considering that Hairless dogs sweat through their skin and feet like humans, any prolonged vomiting or diarrhea can cause dehydration and lead to a more serious condition. Profuse bloody diarrhea must be treated as an emergency.

Hemorrhagic gastroenteritis (HGE) is characterized by an acute onset of bloody diarrhea in formerly healthy and well-cared-for dogs. The cause is unknown. Death can occur fast in untreated dogs. Sometimes HGE is misdiagnosed for parvo and treated with the wrong medicine. If your Crested was vaccinated against parvovirus, yet shows parvo symptoms, you should ask the veterinarian about the possibility of HGE.

Vomiting is caused by irritation of the stomach. Vomiting should not be confused with

An upset tummy is common to curious Cresteds always willing to taste anything that smells interesting.

regurgitation of food shortly after a meal. Unproductive retching for a long period without diarrhea or accompanied by constipation is a danger signal that the dog could have torsion, which can cause death in an hour or less. This condition requires an immediate trip to the emergency clinic. Vomiting after meals can be caused by eating too much too fast. Many Cresteds like to eat grass and vomit it later. This is usually not a cause for concern. Chronic retching and bloody or foul-smelling vomitus, or projectile vomiting, can be the symptoms of more serious problems such as megaesophagus.

Megaesophagus is a rare disease in which the esophagus loses muscle tone, leading to problems swallowing and causing regurgitation in the affected Chinese Crested dogs. The disease is believed to be genetic only in young dogs; in older dogs it is an acquired problem. Dogs can be maintained well for a long time with this disease under medical supervision. Whenever megaesophagus is diagnosed, myasthenia gravis should be suspected (see page 81).

Dogs sometimes develop constipation from eating grass or paper, or swallowing bones. Powderpuffs can be constipated when a soft stool sticks to the long fur around the rectum and blocks the opening. For this reason, a Powderpuff's owner should keep the area around the Crested's rectum shaved.

Why do some Cresteds have nasty doggy breath? In a majority of cases, dental cavities or plaque are at fault. If your Crested's teeth are clean and healthy, then poor digestion is usually the next probable cause of bad breath. Your dog may be struggling to digest her food and the partially digested food could be giving off a foul odor.

Bad gas in Cresteds is another problem resulting from poor digestion. Lack of digestive enzymes can force some Cresteds to start eating their own stool to get needed nutrients. Some Chinese Cresteds can be lactose intolerant. Often, upgrading the dog's diet is sufficient to cure the problem.

Anal gland disease is a frequent problem among Chinese Cresteds. Affected dogs and cats may lick the anal area, "scoot" along the floor, or have problems with defecation. Glands within the anal sacs produce a foul-smelling, greasy material. This material normally is discharged into the bowel movement when the dog defecates. However, retained anal secretions may lead to a serious bacterial infection requiring veterinary help.

Coprophogia, or stool eating, is common in the Chinese Crested. Although the habit looks unpleasant to the owner, to the dog it is, well . . . normal. Occasionally the reason can be found in a dog's poor absorption of nutrients or a physical condition such as diabetes, Cushing's disease, or thyroid disease. However, most Cresteds with an appetite for stools are healthy. Some experts are of the opinion that coprophagy is an instinctual behavior. On the other hand, animal behaviorists claim that it is caused by stress. Yet another view is that dogs engage in this activity because feces have unused proteins and enzymes in them.

Respiratory System

Laryngeal paralysis is a disorder affecting certain Chinese Crested lines, causing difficulty with breathing, and manifests itself as harsh, rasping respiratory sounds, often after exercise or too much excitement. An occasional retching cough and muffled bark are also typical. Sometimes the throat obstruction is so severe that the dog is unable to take more than a few steps at a time without becoming fatigued. The specific cause of the muscle paralysis is not known. The only treatment at the moment for laryngeal paralysis involves surgery.

A collapsed trachea can happen in the Chinese Crested regardless of age. The trachea is a flexible tube that hooks the upper airway to the lower airway and the lungs. When these cartilage rings start to fold in during inhalation or exhalation, the condition is known as a tracheal collapse. The main symptom of a collapsed trachea is a classic honking cough, called a goose-honk cough. The cause of tracheal collapse is unknown. There can be a hereditary implication, particularly if it occurs in younger dogs, but injury to the throat caused by a tight

The exact cause of reverse sneezing
episodes is unknown but possibly
related to allergies.

collar, rough handling, or grabbing by the neck can also be the cause. Collapsed tracheae can be treated medically or surgically, but not always successfully.

"Canine flu" is a new disease that appeared first in 2005. Symptoms include diarrhea, vomiting, a cough, nasal discharge, lethargy, and often a fever. In some dogs, the disease may progress to pneumonia. The virus could possibly be contagious to humans and manifest itself as a stomach virus. The fatality rate among affected dogs is from 1 to 10 percent. Treating canine flu with antibiotics is very effective; timing is crucial, however, as some Chinese Cresteds have been known to die within 24 hours of exhibiting symptoms.

Reverse sneezing is common in Cresteds. In a regular sneeze, your dog pushes air out through the nose; however, in a reverse sneeze, air is pulled rapidly in through the nose. Each reverse sneezing episode generally lasts for less than a minute up to two minutes. A reverse sneeze bout may look alarming but is not life threatening.

Cardiovascular System

Typical signs of heart disease in Chinese Cresteds include weakness, poor appetite, coughing, fainting, difficulty in breathing, enlarged abdomen, pale bluish gums, a rapid, weak heart rate, and pronounced heart murmurs. Abnormal heart rhythm is a typical finding, too.

Endocardiosis is often referred to as mitral valve disease or MVD and usually affects middle-aged and older Cresteds. Dogs with mitral valve disease are often unable to exercise and tend to cough during exertion. Typically, the cough is worse at night, in the morning, and during exertion. It may have a hereditary predisposition.

The most common congenital heart diseases are pulmonic stenosis, valvular stenosis, and patent ductus arteriosis. These problems can eventually lead to congestive heart failure unless repaired by medical specialists. Puppies with serious congenital heart defects usually die soon after birth.

Reproductive System

The heat cycle in Crested females comes usually every six to ten months.

Ovulation in Chinese Crested bitches can take place any time from the second day of the heat to the last day. Some bitches will refuse to stand for the male if they dislike him. Some bitches may come into heat or prolong the heat to breed with the male of their choice.

It must be added that Chinese Crested dogs are very sexually oriented. Many males enjoy having sex just for the pleasure of it, even if they are neutered. Spayed bitches will usually act like males.

Pseudo-pregnancy is common in nonpregnant Crested females. Nonpregnant bitches can show symptoms of true pregnancy, such as weight gain, lactation, vaginal discharge, and nesting behavior. The condition is self-limiting, usually regressing in three to five weeks. Therapy is not necessary unless the symptoms are prolonged beyond the normal pregnancy time.

Normal pregnancy lasts from 57 to 70 days. It is common in Hairless bitches to reabsorb the

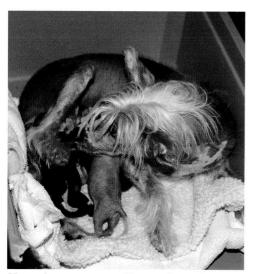

Normal pregnancy in Chinese Cresteds lasts from 57 to 70 days.

Spaying is the surgical removal of the reproductive organs of the female animal to prevent breeding or for health reasons.

dead fetus or embryo without expulsion from the uterus. Some puppies can also be born dead. Lethal genes present in Hairless Cresteds will cause death in one-fourth of Hairless puppies conceived of two Hairless parents. Some fetuses are born deformed. On occasion, a disease of the reproductive system such as brucella canis is the cause of a miscarriage of fetuses at about 45 to 59 days. The grayish-green discharge associated with the miscarriage is toxic, and touching it should be avoided. Affected bitches must undergo antibiotic therapy and be isolated from other dogs.

Dystocia is difficulty in delivery of a puppy through the birth canal. If a bitch has been in labor for more than four hours without giving birth, or two hours or more have passed between births while the bitch strains having contractions, veterinary help is advised. Sometimes a C-section is the only option. Most Crested bitches recuperate fast after a C-section; however, puppies may be affected by the anesthesia and die soon after birth.

Herpesvirus is one of the most common reproductive syndromes responsible for neonatal mortality. The bitch usually appears healthy. There is no cure, and the next litters are usually not affected. Keeping the dam and newborns on a warm pillow sometimes helps them avoid the infection.

Eclampsia most commonly occurs one to three weeks after giving birth, but it can also occur during pregnancy. It is also called milk fever or puerperal tetany, and is an acute, life-threatening disease caused by low blood calcium levels (hypocalcemia) in dogs. Lactating females are particularly susceptible to blood calcium depletion because of milk production and nursing. At first, the dam will act restless and nervous. Very soon, she will walk with a stiff, unbalanced gait and may appear disoriented. Eventually, she may be unable to walk. There is usually a high fever over 105°F (41°C). Veterinary attention must be sought at once and the puppies prevented from nursing for at least 24 hours. Death can occur without fast treatment.

Metritis, an acute postpartum infection of the uterus, should be suspected if lethargy, fever, anorexia, and ill-smelling thick, tomato-like color discharge is seen in the mother. Sometimes spaying a bitch is the only option to save her life. Nursing puppies should be removed and raised by hand until the mother's condition sufficiently improves.

Mastitis is an inflammation of the mammary glands in Crested bitches either after the parturition or in false pregnancy. Warm compresses and a gentle massage of the inflamed breast is often all that is required.

Vaginal infection is also common in Crested bitches. The Crested female may show vulvar discharge accompanied by licking and attraction from male dogs. Juvenile vaginitis is common in puppy bitches. The condition usually resolves naturally after the first estrous heat. In rare cases, antibiotic therapy is advised.

The normal Crested male should have two testicles descended to the scrotum by eight weeks, although on occasion the process may take up to six months. Monorchism describes a condition in which a male dog has only one testicle, and cryptorchidism is when both testicles are missing. These defects are considered hereditary.

Neutering or castration is the surgical removal of the reproductive glands (testes) of the male dog. Chinese Crested dogs should be spayed or neutered by the sixth to seventh month to prevent development of unpleasant habits. In males, neutering eliminates the chances of developing testicular cancer. It also reduces problems associated with nasty male behaviors, such as aggression and marking. In females, spaying decreases the incidence of breast cancer and eliminates the chance of developing pyometria, a potentially fatal infection of the uterus.

Urinary Problems

Signs of urinary infection or stones include frequent licking of the urethra, incontinence or dribbling urine, blood in the urine, increased need to urinate, and increased thirst. A dog may walk arching its back. A urine sample is required to properly diagnose and treat bladder infection.

Incontinence usually occurs in the older spayed bitch or in young puppies. In older dogs, it is often caused by a hormonal imbalance and as such can be easily treated. Most puppies outgrow the problem by the time they turn nine months old. If it becomes a problem, a Crested should be dressed in doggy pants containing a pad to absorb the urine.

Kidney failure happens because of poisonings, changes in blood flow to the kidney, obstructions, infections, congenital defects, and, very rarely, for no apparent reason.

Bone Fractures and Skeletal Defects

The majority of Chinese Cresteds, particularly of the Hairless variety, love to climb, jump, and leap, often without giving these activities a second thought. Therefore, broken legs are rather common. In addition to a broken leg, the Crested may also suffer a pelvic fracture if she falls on a hard surface. Although most fractures of the pelvis heal perfectly well with little treatment other than simple rest, there can be complications at times, so the dog's pelvis needs to be X-rayed to check if it is healing properly. Acquired dislocation is the result of direct trauma to the shoulder region.

Patellar luxation, or dislocating kneecaps, can be inherited or acquired through trauma and can occur sporadically in the Chinese Cresteds. The signs of patellar luxation are difficulty in straightening the knee, walking on three legs, inability to bear weight on the affected leg, pain in the stifle, and/or a limp. In severe cases,

Broken limbs, from climbing or jumping, are common in the Chinese Crested, so exercise should be done on a flat, even surface.

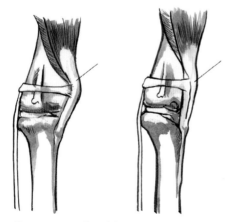

Patellas in normal and luxating position.

corrective surgery is the only help for a luxating patella problem.

Osteochondrosis is an abnormality in the normal development of bones. The first symptoms appear when the dog becomes unable to climb or come down steps.

Arthritis mainly affects older Cresteds. Common clinical signs include limping, inability or reluctance to climb stairs, difficulty getting up, stiffness, and licking of a joint. Most veterinarians will prescribe pain-controlling or anti-inflammatory drugs.

Skin Problems and Care

The skin of the Hairless Crested is composed of more than one layer, so it is thicker and less delicate than the skin of the Powderpuff or any other dog. The major problem affecting the Chinese Hairless Crested is acne and blackheads that, when neglected, can lead to severe bacterial infection and inflammation. Some hairless dogs may also benefit from being regularly treated with hydroxyl alpha cream or lotion. Selsun Blue shampoo or Sebulex Medicated 2–2% Shampoo have a drying effect and are excellent remedies for infected skin, seborrhea, acne, and in treating oily skin in the Hairless Crested and dandruff in Powderpuffs. Sulfur soap from Stiffel can be also used to improve skin appearance. Since some Cresteds can be allergic to sulfur, caution is advised when attempting any sulfur therapy.

Bacterial and yeast infections are common to Hairless Crested dogs. They may show up as tiny bumps usually filled with puss and accompanied by larger abscesses. Occasionally, a Crested can be also infected with ringworm or mange; however, these diseases attack mostly the Powderpuffs.

Preventive care is the key to healthy skin, especially because a cure is time consuming, requires much effort, and is not always successful. Poor hygiene results in bad-smelling skin, acne, and bacterial infection.

If your Chinese Crested Hairless lives in a sunny climate, you should apply sunscreen to her skin when going out. Considering that the dog perspires, keeping her too long in the sun can cause dehydration and sunstroke. During hot summer days, she needs to be in a cool room, always with plenty of water to drink. Dogs living in cold climates need to be dressed warmly to prevent them from catching pneumonia. Playing in the snow can be fun; however, the feet are delicate and can suffer frost injury. If your dog must walk on the ice, getting a pair of warm boots is a great idea.

How to Remove Blackheads

To remove blackheads, the skin needs to be scrubbed well first with an iodine-based shampoo. Holding the dog under the warm running water, squeeze the pores gently but firmly to discharge puss and expel the retained hair roots. Warm water desensitizes the dog to pain, allowing you to cleanse the skin. After the procedure, the dog has to be washed again with the iodine shampoo and dried thoroughly either with a towel or a blow dryer. Once the skin is dry, a thin film of non-oily antibiotic cream should be applied. This will help heal the skin faster and prevent the spreading of bacteria and reinfection.

Balneotherapy

Mineral salts used in baths seem to cure acne, eczema, dandruff, and infected hair follicles, which are often the cause of nasty boils in the

It is not an exaggeration to say that most skin problems result from owner neglect or taking things for granted.

Hairless Crested. Starch or oatmeal baths are the best for inflamed skin. The bath formulas below can benefit not only the dog, but the owner, too. Water temperature should not be hotter than 97°F (36°C).

Soda Bath: Dissolve 1 pound (454 g) of baking soda in a full tub of water (30 gallons [115 L]). A ten-minute soak is antiseptic, and relieves itching and skin irritation. Good for conditions such as hives or bug bites.

Starch or Oatmeal Bath: Add 1 pound (454 g) of dry cornstarch or finely ground oatmeal to a full tub of water (30 gallons [115 L]). A 15-minute soak acts as a cooling agent, relieving skin irritations and itchiness from such conditions as poison ivy, poison oak, eczema, and sunburn.

Brine Bath: Add 5.5–6.5 pounds (2.5–3 kg) of common salt or, better yet, Dead Sea salt crystals, to a bathtub of hot water and allow it to cool to a temperature of 95°F (35°C). A salt bath is taken to open the pores and cleanse the skin from blackheads. Because the salt acts as a stimulant, resulting in profuse sweating, the bath should be very short, not longer than five minutes. After the bath, the dog is wrapped in a warm blanket to continue the sweating while the owner tries to remove the blackheads and retained hair roots from the skin.

Allergies

Chinese Cresteds get allergies, no question about it! Symptoms of allergy are itchiness, scratching, chewing or gnawing at the skin,

Example of micropthalmia: one eye is smaller than the other.

excessive licking, rash or skin eruptions, hot spots, and hair loss.

Food sensitivities in the Chinese Crested are most commonly linked with skin problems. Cresteds can be allergic to various ingredients commonly found in dog foods, such as corn, soy, or lamb. A dog that has been fed the same diet for years and has always seemed healthy can suddenly develop allergy symptoms and no longer tolerate the food. In this case, a change of diet is all that is needed.

Contact allergies tend to be the least common kind. Examples include a reaction to a flea collar, topical ointment, or certain bedding materials such as wool or foam.

An inhalant allergy is an allergy to substances such as dust mites, pollen, mildew, and mold.

TIP

Shampoo

Use gentle shampoo specifically formulated for dogs. Irritants such as shampoo may cause your Crested to scratch her eye, which in turn may lead to ulcers. Put a small amount of eye lubricant in your dog's eyes before giving her a bath!

They may be bothering your Crested if she is licking her paws or under her legs in the armpit area or around the groin. These allergens can also cause chronic ear infections, so if your dog is shaking her head a lot, she may be suffering from an inhalant allergy. Introducing to the Crested's diet essential fatty acids, such as omega-3 and omega-6 oils, which can be purchased at most pet stores, can sometimes resolve the allergy problem without medical intervention.

Eye Disorders

Chinese Cresteds can suffer from a variety of eye problems. Dry eye, glaucoma, lens luxation, juvenile cataracts, and progressive retinopathy are the most common disorders affecting the breed.

A cataract is a clouding of the lens of the eye. Cataracts in Chinese Cresteds can develop early or late. Once they become mature, they will cause blindness. They can affect one or both eyes. To save the Crested's vision, surgical removal of cataracts done before a cataract matures is the best course of action.

Glaucoma in dogs is classified as either primary or secondary. Primary glaucoma is an inherited condition. It usually begins in one eye, but usually eventually involves both eyes, leading to complete blindness. Secondary glaucoma occurs often because of the dry-eye condition. Because glaucoma causes a chronic headache, it is important to have your Crested examined by a veterinary ophthalmologist as soon as possible.

Progressive retinal atrophy (PRA) in Chinese Cresteds is another genetic disorder affecting vision. This is an inherited disease of the retina, which occurs in both eyes at the same time. Although there is no cure for it, the condition is not painful. Clinical signs vary from the dog

How to Administer Eye Drops

An easy way to administer eye drops to your Crested is to stand behind the dog while holding the eye open to administer the drops or the ointment.

becoming night blind in the early stage to complete blindness. It is believed that nutritional antioxidant supplementation, such as SOD, may slow the deterioration of the retina. SOD is Superoxide Disomutase and is a potent anti-inflammatory and also one of the most powerful naturally-occuring antioxidants in animals and humans. It can be found in most health food stores and pharmacies. Note that PRA in Chinese Cresteds appears to consist of at least two different genetic defects. A Chinese Crested of known status for prcd-PRA could still be at risk for another, yet unidentified, form of PRA. A CERF examination can detect eye problems long before they become obvious and consists of a simple and painless test performed by an ophthalmologist approved by the Canine Eye Registry Foundation.

Chronic corneal erosions are eye wounds caused by some trauma that fail to heal and can persist for many weeks or months.

Cherry eye (PTEG) is another ophthalmologic condition that can affect Cresteds. Dogs have a third eyelid that slides up over the surface of the eye for protection. Some dogs are born with weak ligaments, which allow the TEG, or third eyelid gland, to pop out of its normal position, resulting in something that looks like a large pink, round pimple in the inside corner of the eye. The condition can be in one eye or both eyes. Treatment is surgical. If the condition is left untreated, the eye is at risk for developing dry eye.

Eye abnormalities affect mostly the Chinese Crested Hairless.

Some hairless puppies can be born with micropthalmia, which is a defect of one abnormally small eye. The defect is believed to be of genetic origin.

Ear Problems

A Crested may also be unilaterally deaf, bilaterally deaf, or bilaterally hearing. The only way to be certain of a dog's hearing status is to have its hearing tested by a BAER test (Brainstem Auditory Evoked Response).

Occasionally a Hairless Crested will be born with missing ear canals. This defect is common in all hairless breeds. A Crested dog with missing ear canals should not be bred, as the condition is most likely hereditary.

If the skin inside the ear is inflamed and you detect a foul odor or discharge, or the Crested shakes her head and paws at the ears, she may have an ear infection. The most common causes of ear problems are yeast, bacterial infections, or mites. A more serious condition will need to be treated by a doctor.

Teeth Care

Hairless Crested dogs usually do not have normal teeth. They have many missing teeth, and the teeth they have may grow at odd angles or be crooked. The canines frequently grow forward like tusks. The roots of the teeth can be abnormally short. Powderpuff Chinese Crested dogs should have a complete dentition.

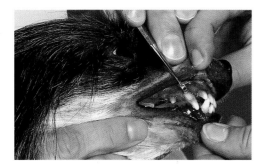

Crested Hairless dogs usually have missing teeth and tusk-like canines.

Periodontal disease and cavities are the most common causes of early tooth loss. To prevent periodontal disease, you need to brush your pet's teeth frequently and not allow your dog to chew on hard toys or bones.

Regular periodontal cleaning to remove plaque and tartar will assist in maintaining clean teeth. There are also home dental programs such as LEBA III, which can be successfully used by the average pet owner.

Malocclusion is the deformation of a dog's jaw structure, leaving either the lower jaw or the upper jaw out of line, or occasionally the increased growth of a single side of a jaw, causing a wry mouth. This is a relatively rare occurrence. Overshot bite, also known as parrot mouth, happens when the upper jaw extends beyond the lower jaw. Undershot bite occurs when the lower jaw protrudes out past the upper jaw. Both overshot and undershot bites are considered faults in the Chinese Crested breed.

Other Common Disorders

Cushing's disease results when the adrenal glands produce excessive amounts of cortisol, a hormone with potent anti-inflammatory and immunosuppressive effects. The disease is commonly seen in middle-aged and older dogs. The signs of Cushing's include excessive drinking and urination, tiredness, a potbellied abdomen, chronic infections, and hair loss. Some Cresteds develop skin rash, or itchy, scaly skin lesions, suffer seizures, and develop diabetes. Prolonged administration of cortisone may cause Cushing's in susceptible dogs. There is no cure, only a method of extending longevity. The average lifespan of dogs that have had Cushing's diagnosed, with treatment, is estimated at two years.

Addison's disease is caused by the adrenal glands producing a lower-than-normal amount of hormones, such as hydrocortisone and aldosterone. Addison's disease affects usually young to middle-aged dogs; signs may appear suddenly or gradually and may include weakness, low body temperature, depression, loss of appetite, irregular heart rate, weak pulses, vomiting, diarrhea, and sometimes increased thirst and copious urine production. Cresteds suffering from Addison's disease are unable to deal with stress, and the symptoms may worsen whenever they become upset or stressed.

Diabetes also occurs in Cresteds. Diabetes mellitus is the most clinically recognized form of diabetes in dogs and is generally referred to as sugar diabetes. The initial symptoms usually consist of excessive drinking and urination. When present in puppies, diabetes often results in a failure to grow properly. Some puppies may become too weak to eat or drink. The treatment involves daily insulin injections. Four or more smaller meals are preferred over one large meal. Juvenile hypoglycemia, or low blood sugar, is very common in puppies, too, particularly undersized puppies. The disorder occurs mainly

Many of the Chinese Crested's health problems are hereditary.

in puppies between 6 and 12 weeks of age. The first signs are listlessness and depression, followed later by muscular weakness, convulsions, and coma.

Liver shunt, or a portosystemic shunt (PSS), refers to abnormal blood flow in the liver. The clinical signs associated with PSS are often neurological, like epilepsy. Liver shunt is a serious defect. Unfortunately, only certain shunts can be corrected surgically.

Epilepsy has been found to affect certain family lines of the Chinese Crested. An epileptic seizure is the clinical manifestation of abnormal brain activity in the brain's cortex. Several types of seizures are known to affect dogs, and sometimes owners are not even aware that their dogs are having an attack. Some forms of epilepsy are hereditary. There is no cure for epilepsy, but with good care and medicine, the disorder can usually be controlled, depending on cause and severity.

Myasthenia gravis is a neuromuscular disease whose primary sign is weakness. This weakness leads to problems in swallowing and is a cause of regurgitation. It may also lead to inhalation pneumonia. It is often linked to megaesophagus disease and should be suspected whenever megaesophagus is present.

FIRST AID FOR THE CHINESE CRESTED

What should you do if it is the middle of the night and the nearest pet emergency care is hours away?

Emergencies

Home treatment does not take the place of veterinary care. This guide is to be used only in situations when you cannot get immediate help for your Crested and time is of the essence.

Shock

Major symptoms of anaphylactic shock are staggering gait, weak pulse, clammy skin, and pale gums. Shock can result from an allergic reaction to an insect bite, trauma, medication, or a recent vaccine injection.

The Crested should be immediately treated with an antihistamine such as Benadryl. The adult dose is ¾ to 1 dropper full, and for puppies about ¼ to ½ dropper full. (A dropper full usually consists of 30 drops.) Next, raise the dog's temperature to normal by placing him on a hot pillow set at medium heat or next to

Quick action in an emergency can save your dog's life.

a hot water bottle. The head should be held lower than the heart. Gently massage the limbs to bring back circulation. The dog should show signs of improvement within 15 minutes. If he does not, another, slightly smaller dose of Benadryl (about ½ dropper full) should bring the dog back to normal. Once the dog is in stable condition, he should be transported as soon as possible to the nearest veterinary hospital for evaluation.

Heat Stroke

Signs of heat stroke include excessive panting, rapid heartbeat, vomiting, diarrhea, and unconsciousness. Treatment must be immediate and requires lowering the body temperature with cool water immersion and placing ice packs on the head to keep the body temperature stable.

Poisonous Mushrooms

If the Crested digests any poisonous mushrooms, the quick recommendation is to induce

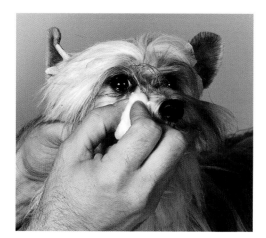

vomiting by using syrup of ipecac, followed by the intake of activated charcoal. It takes about 1 teaspoon (5 mL) of ipecac syrup per 10 pounds (4.5 kg) of body weight to induce vomiting, on the average. Because overdosage can cause heart problems, these directions must be followed in detail.

Venomous Snakebite

There is no home remedy for a poisonous snakebite. The only thing that can be done is to make the dog comfortable while transporting him to the nearest hospital. The dog must be kept calm and his movements restricted. The affected area should be kept below heart level to reduce the flow of venom. If the dog is unable to reach medical care within 30 minutes, a bandage, wrapped 2 to 4 inches (5–10 cm) above the bite, may help slow the venom. The bandage should be loose enough so that a finger can slip under it, so as not to cut off blood flow from the artery. A suction device may be placed over the bite to help draw venom out of the wound. If such a device is unavailable, mouth suction can be applied

instead. If the poison is swallowed, the stomach will inactivate it. Applying ice to the wound will only make matters worse.

Hypoglycemic Shock

Hypoglycemia is a condition in which there is a drastic, sudden drop in a dog's level of blood sugar. The dog will go into shock and, if not cared for properly, will die. If your Chinese Crested puppy shows symptoms of hypoglycemia, fast action is necessary. The puppy should be immediately given a teaspoon (5 mL) of corn syrup by mouth, followed by a teaspoon (5 mL) of Pedialyte. The best way to do this for a tiny puppy is to open his mouth and deposit a drop of syrup on his tongue, then close the mouth and wait until it is swallowed. In this way, a full amount of corn syrup and Pedialyte, drop by drop, should be provided. If a puppy does not improve in 30 minutes, the situation must be considered an emergency, because without immediate medical help, the puppy will die.

Note: To prevent future hypoglycemia attacks in tiny puppies, they should never be allowed to play longer than 15 minutes at a time. Play must be followed by feeding, forceful if necessary, and then sleep or rest. The puppy should be kept warm and dry, and provided with plenty of water, perhaps some goat's milk and tasty, high-energy snacks. Giving the puppy ½ teaspoon

Ethnobotanists suggest that adding a small pinch of cinnamon (Cinnamomum zeylanicum) to food may help control blood sugar levels.

Chinese Crested puppies can get anaphylactic shock from a vaccine injection.

(2 mL) of Nutrical or Stat every morning and night will help him maintain necessary energy. For hypoglycemic puppies, at least six feedings a day are recommended, and if the puppy refuses food, he must be force-fed by hand.

Swallowing Glass, Tacks, or Staples

If your Crested eats small pieces of glass, tacks, small nails, or staples, he can be treated at home with a "cream and cotton balls" formula. The cotton balls must be real cotton, not the cosmetic kind made from synthetic fibers. The balls need to be soaked in the cream until soggy and then put into a freezer. They should become semi-hard in ten minutes or so. Once

frozen, they must be fed to the Crested as follows: Dogs less than 10 pounds (4.5 kg) should eat two balls cut into smaller pieces. Dogs 10–50 pounds (4.5–22.5 kg) should eat three to five whole balls, and larger dogs should have five to seven. As the cotton works its way through the digestive tract, it will find all the glass pieces or a staple and wrap itself around them, protecting the intestines from potentially serious damage. The cotton always comes out with the object safely embedded.

Diarrhea and Vomiting

In the case of diarrhea or vomiting, an immediate fast is recommended to rest the digestive

Prevent hypoglycemia in your puppy with frequent meals.

tract. Pedialyte electrolyte baby formula, which is readily available in supermarkets or gas stations, should be offered to treat dehydration. It is given by mouth at the rate of 2 to 4 cc per pound of body weight per hour, depending upon the severity of the dehydration. A formula consisting of a tablespoon (15 mL) of cornstarch and a teaspoon (5 mL) of freshly squeezed lime juice added to a cup of water has been found very helpful in treating intestinal inflammation in adults and young puppies. A warm pillow put over the Crested's tummy will help him to cope with stomach spasms. If the Crested does not improve in 12 hours, he should be seen by a veterinarian at the first opportunity to determine the cause.

Broken Leg

Wrapping broken legs is easy and requires keeping only a few supplies on hand. A tempo-

rary splint can be made from a folded newspaper or a 2-inch (5-cm) plastic pipe that is split into thirds; even a toilet paper roll will do. The splint is filled evenly with cotton padding, and the rough edges are either ground with a file or cut away. The broken limb is placed on a table and set as straight as possible, then wrapped once or twice in cotton (it comes in rolls) to add extra padding, and then in a surgical gauze (a 4-inch [10-cm] size is best), and finally, secured with duct tape. Because the leg will swell after the injury, the bandage should be loose enough so that a finger can slip under it. A pet medical collar should be placed around the dog's neck to prevent it from removing the bandage.

The Crested must be transported to the hospital as soon as possible for further treatment or surgery.

Home Remedies

Some health problems can be safely treated at home. However, if the Crested does not improve within a few days, it may mean more serious problems and you should seek professional help.

Constipation

Adding 1/8 teaspoon (.5 g) per meal of Metamucil or other fiber to soft food for each 5–10 pounds (2.2–4.5 kg) of body weight will prevent constipation in most Cresteds. Another great way to prevent constipation is to add pumpkin to the Crested's dry food. Most Crested dogs love the taste of canned pumpkin, about 1 to 1½ teaspoons (5–7 g) per meal.

Some health problems can be safely treated at home.

Bad Gas

A teaspoon (5 g) of low-fat yogurt with each meal or a powdered yucca root (⅓ capsule with every meal) should help reduce internal gas.

Reverse Sneezing

An attack can be stopped by massaging the dog's throat or nose.

Ear Infection

A good home remedy to treat simple infections is provided in this formula:

1 Tbs. (15 mL) boric acid
2 oz. (60 mL) rubbing alcohol
1½ tsp. (7 mL) glycerin

All ingredients should be mixed well and shaken before each use. Putting a few drops into each ear and rubbing gently should soothe the inflammation. After a few minutes, the ears need to be cleaned with cotton swabs. In addition, a small amount of hydrogen peroxide warmed and poured inside the dog's ears will dislocate most wax and dirt and remove any unpleasant odor. A bit of cotton should be put inside the ear to dry the moisture.

Impacted Anal Glands

When the anal glands become impacted, the Crested's owner must clean them out by expressing the contents. This is done by applying pressure with the finger below the gland and then pushing it upwards.

Coprophogia: The best method to prevent the problem is to keep your dog's area free of feces by removing it immediately. Sometimes adding digestive enzymes to the Crested's diet may cure this unpleasant problem.

OLD AGE

Chinese Cresteds generally age very gracefully, retaining their physical and mental abilities until the very last. These dogs love life! It is not uncommon to see a Crested still jumping merrily and chasing a ball at 14 or 15 years of age.

The Aging Chinese Crested

The biggest problem is the Crested Hairless dog's poor dentition and progressive tooth loss, which can start very early in life. Because crunching and chewing dry foods can be too troublesome or even painful for the toothless dog, you should feed your Crested soft foods with added chopped vegetables and fruit, or add a vitamin and mineral supplement to the diet to make sure the senior gets enough calories and nutrition.

Occasionally Hairless Cresteds who have lost their teeth may end up with their tongue hanging out one side of their mouths. Although unusual looking, this does not interfere with eating habits, nor does it cause any health issues.

Many old Chinese Cresteds suffer from cataracts. These dogs need to be treated with

Most Chinese Cresteds age very gracefully and love life to the very end.

kindness and patience. If they must to go outside at night, they should be let out with another companion and in a well-lighted area.

Arthritis is another problem affecting elder Cresteds. Cresteds suffering from arthritis can have difficulty walking or getting up. These dogs need soft beds to feel comfortable and food bowls at head level so that they will not have to bend down to eat or drink.

Incontinence can easily be dealt with by dressing the pet in padded panties made especially for urine-dripping dogs.

Most Chinese Crested males retain their fertility to the end, but females come into menopause relatively early, around eight years or younger. Nevertheless, there are known cases of older bitches getting pregnant and having healthy litters at 10 or 11 years of age. The strain of pregnancy on their bodies is too heavy, however, and the chance of complications and pyrometra is too high to risk breeding them. It

Make your beloved pal comfortable in his final years.

dogs do not get wrinkles; however, they often suffer from lipomas, which are benign fatty tumors; papillomas; and occasionally skin cancers, including the malignant form.

Breast cancer is also common among unspayed elderly females, and older males get prostate cancer regardless of whether or not they are neutered.

is much safer and healthier to spay them once they reach seven or eight years of age.

Many owners of Chinese Crested Hairless dogs wonder about the skin. Does it get wrinkles like the skin on humans? The answer is no. Hairless

Some older Crested dogs suffer from senility and can act confused or disoriented. Special attention is required for such dogs and, if necessary, a drug therapy.

The Rainbow Bridge

No words can adequately express the suffering that many Crested owners undergo upon the passing of their beloved companion.

Chinese Cresteds are known to have a great emotional and bonding effect, and when they have to leave for the Rainbow Bridge, their owners who have loved them so dearly are often left in a terrible shock. In fact, the sense of loss can be so overwhelming that many want to immediately seek a replacement in the hope of finding another Crested that is as identical as possible to the one that has just died.

The futility of this idea is obvious. No dog can replace the passed-away companion, as every dog is different and has a different personality. Even if the dog looks the same, expectations of "sameness" are doomed to fail, often hurting the owner and the new pet in the process. In all earnestness, it is better to WAIT, and then once the period of grief is over, seek a different-looking dog and prepare for a different experience.

*"Farewell my best friend! There was
no love more genuine than yours."*

Another issue that needs to be addressed is
the final resting place for the deceased pet. A
popular custom in the United States is crema-
tion or laying the body in a casket and burying
it in either a pet cemetery or one's garden. The
burials, like those for humans, are often ceremo-
nial. The cost is about $300 for a smaller dog
like a Chinese Crested. The pet's ashes can be
also kept at home in a decorative funeral urn.

In Memory of Lulu

She was my little butterfly
Soft wings of the night
Wet flame of the morning
Daily cup of living waters
That the Lady of Flowers broke
Emerging through the thin ice of time
Around my heart entwining
Long bloodless fingers
White like a rose
She had blossomed

—Anna Morton

INFORMATION

References

Baus de Czitrom, Carolyn. 1988. *Los perros de la antigua provincia de Colima.* Colección Catálogos de Museos. INAH.

Cardew, Mirrie, 1986. *A Chinese Crested Dog for Me.* Midland Counties Publications, U.K.

Duncan, Barbara R. and Brett H. Riggs. 2003. *Cherokee Heritage Trails Guidebook.* Chapel Hill: University of North Carolina Press.

Fernandez, Amy, and Kelly Rhae, 1998/9. *Hairless Dogs—The Naked Truth.* U.S.A.

Jones, Brenda, 1990. *Book of the Breed—The Complete Chinese Crested,* Ringpress, U.K.

Pryor, Karen, 2005. *Getting Started: Clicker Training for Dogs (Getting Started),* Sunshine Books.

Sahagun, Fray Bernardino de. 1979. *Historia general de las cosas de Nueva España,* A. M. Garibay K., Col. Sepan Cuantos número 300, Editorial Porrúa, México.

Sanchez Martinez, Fernando. 1994. Ponencia "Rescate, identificación y conservación del-material orgánico arqueológico: La cueva "El Gallo," Ticumán, Morelos." XXIII Mesa Redonda de la Sociedad Mexicana de Antropología.

Tellington-Jones, Linda, 2001. *Getting in Touch with Your Dog: A Gentle Approach to Influencing Behavior, Health, Performance.* Trafalgar Square Publishing.

Van der Lyn, Edita, 1964. *How to Raise and Train a Chinese Crested.* Jersey City, T F H Publications.

Organizations

American Chinese Crested Club, Inc.
Corresponding Secretary: Marian Blackman
1102 SW 30th Street
Palm City, FL 34990
www.chinesecrestedclub.info

American Kennel Club
Corporate Headquarters
260 Madison Avenue
New York, NY 10016
Operations
5580 Centerview Drive
Raleigh, NC 27606
www.akc.org

Federation Cynologique Internationale
Secretariat General
13, Place Albert I
B6530 Thiun, Belgium
FCI Standard no. 234 / 22.05.1995 / E

Genetic Registry for Hairless Dogs
http://home.znet.com/hairlessdogs/7reg.html

Chinese Crested E-zine
www.chinesecrestedezine.com

Je T'aime Originals
Ultra comfort in dog wear
(pj's, T-shirts, and pee pads)
http://www.jetaimeoriginals.com

Powderpuffs can be mistaken for the Havanese or the Shih-Tzu.

INDEX

About the Author

Anna Morton has been an active Chinese Crested fancier and breeder since 1988, producing many top winning dogs in confirmation and obedience in the U.S. and abroad. The Babylon Cresteds have also distinguished themselves as valuable therapy and guide dogs for sick or disabled persons, and some even became credited with saving their owners' lives. She is also the breeder of a famous Hairless Crested dog 'Eerek', the mascot of Dr. Fitzgerald on the well known TV show Animal Planet, which has entertained millions of children and adults worldwide. Anna Morton is also a writer and a poet and currently resides in Tucson, AZ.

Acknowledgments

The author wishes to express her gratitude to all the people who have made this project possible, but in particular to Wayne Barr for giving her the opportunity to write this book, Miroslaw Lipinski for offering his superb linguistic skills, Andrzej Pastuszek for his financial support, Patricia Weissleader for allowing the use of her extensive archives, Charlotte Ventura for sharing her knowledge of training the Chinese Crested, and Caron Dollar for her diet tips.

Important Note

The Chinese Crested is one of the most intelligent and elegant dogs. However, due to its sensitivity to its environment and intensive grooming requirements, they may not be suitable for every home, particularly the Hairless variety. You need to seriously consider the breeds' demands before deciding on the Crested as your next pet.

The advice given in the book primarily concerns normally developed puppies from a good breeder in excellent physical condition and of good character.

Anyone who adopts a fully grown dog should be aware that the animal has already formed its basic impression of human beings. The new owner should watch the animal carefully, including its behavior toward humans, and should meet the previous owner.

Caution is further advised in the association of children with dogs, in meeting with other dogs, and in exercising the dog without a leash.

Photo Credits

Isabelle Francais: page 2–3, 4, 11, 19, 24, 27, 30, 31 (top left, right), 32, 34, 35, 36, 37, 42, 45, 46, 47, 49, 56, 57, 58, 60, 62, 64, 65, 67, 69, 76, 80, 81, 83, 84, 85, 89, 93; Pets by Paulette: page 6, 7, 9, 10, 17, 23, 25, 86, 88; Tara Darling: page 5, 12, 13, 16, 20, 29, 31 (bottom), 33, 38, 50, 54, 74, 91; Cheryl Ertelt: page 41, 55, 90; Norvia Behling: page 8, 22, 40, 63, 71, 82, 87.

Cover Photos

Front and inside front cover: Pets by Paulette; Back cover: Norvia Behling; Inside back cover: Cheryl Ertelt.

All inquiries should be addressed to:
Barron's Educational Series, Inc.
250 Wireless Boulevard
Hauppauge, NY 11788
www.barronseduc.com

ISBN-13: 978-0-7641-3540-8
ISBN-10: 0-7641-3540-6

Library of Congress Catalog Card No. 2006016404

Library of Congress Cataloging-in-Publication Data
Morton, Anna.
    Chinese crested : everything about purchase, care, quality, nutrition, care, and training / Anna Morton ; filled with full color photographs ; illustrations by Michele Earle-Bridges.
        p. cm. — (A complete pet owner's manual)
    Includes bibliographical references.
    ISBN-13: 978-0-7641-3540-8
    ISBN-10: 0-7641-3540-6
    1. Chinese crested dog. I. Title. II. Series.

SF429.C477M67 2007
636.76—dc22   2006016404

Printed in China
9 8 7 6 5 4 3 2 1